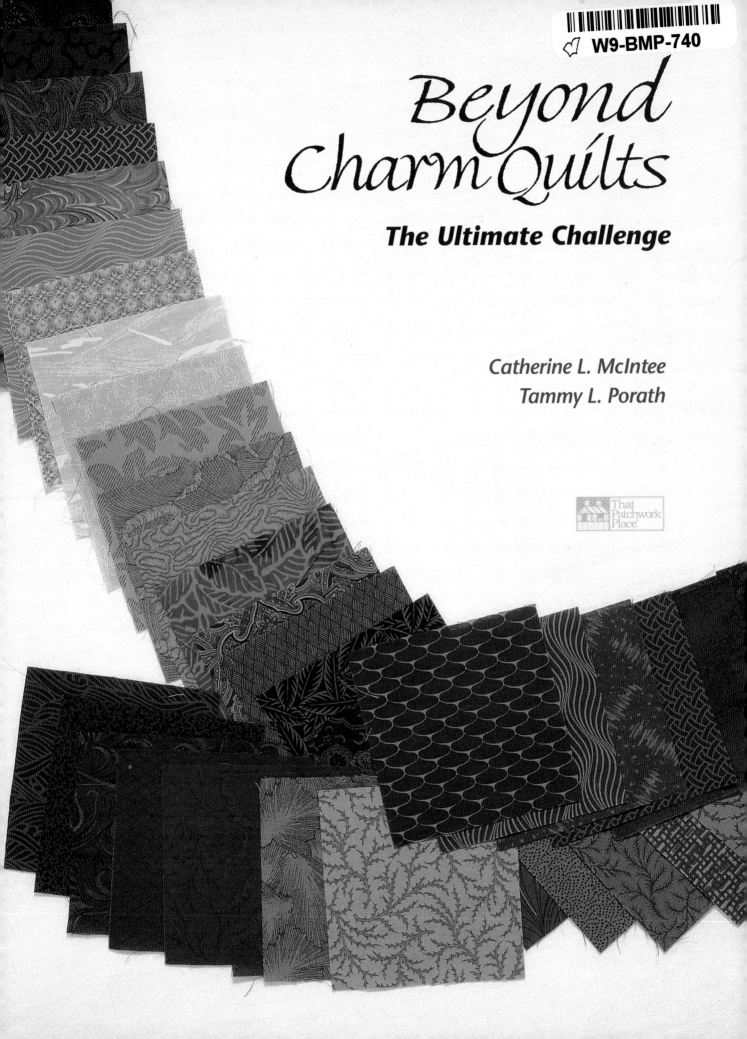

Beyond Charm Quilts

The Ultimate Challenge

Catherine L. McIntee

Tammy L. Porath

That Patchwork Place

Beyond Charm Quilts: The Ultimate Challenge

©1997 by Catherine L. McIntee and Tammy L. Porath

That Patchwork Place, Inc.
PO Box 118
Bothell, WA 98041-0118 USA

Printed in Hong Kong
02 01 00 99 98 97   6 5 4 3 2 1

Library of Congress Cataloging-in-Publication Data

McIntee, Catherine L.,
    Beyond charm quilts : the ultimate challenge / Catherine L. McIntee and Tammy L. Porath.
        p.   cm.
    ISBN 1-56477-174-1
    1. Patchwork—Patterns. 2. Quilting—Patterns. I. Porath, Tammy L. II. Title.
TT835.M279 1997
746. 46'041—dc20   96-30982
                                                       CIP

Dedication

We dedicate this book to all the quilters who produce quilts for the sheer joy of it. We salute the everyday quilters who make no political statement and whose quilts have no deep symbolic meaning. We cheer for the quilters who simply love color, design, and fabric.

Credits

Editor-in-Chief .... Kerry I. Hoffman
Technical Editor .... Ursula Reikes
Managing Editor .... Judy Petry
Copy Editor .... Tina Cook
Proofreader .... Melissa Riesland
Design Director .... Cheryl Stevenson
Text and Cover Designer .... Sandy Wing
Production Assistants .... Claudia L'Heureux, Marijane Figg
Illustrators .... Laurel Strand, Robin Strobel
Photographer .... Brent Kane

Table of Contents

Introduction

We used to be normal people. We were quilters, that's true, but we had a handle on it. That is, until an idea for a quilt project came into our lives. It seemed simple at first, then we played with the idea, and it got more involved. Each step took us further down the path, and before we knew it, almost three years had passed.

The Ultimate Challenge started with the combination of two intriguing concepts—charm quilts and fabric challenges. We mixed these ideas, modified them, and gave them a new slant by working in a series. Ultimate Challenge quilts contain a palette of charm fabrics, but are not charm quilts in the strictest sense of the word because they contain an array of other fabrics as well. They are challenge quilts, but instead of containing one or two challenge fabrics, they have many. When working in a series is added to this mix, you end up with a unique experience called the Ultimate Challenge.

Our adventure started with a packet of charm squares. For those who aren't familiar with the term, a charm quilt is one in which each piece is cut from a different fabric. Most commonly, charm pieces are all the same shape—triangles, squares, hexagons, and so on.

Charm quilts are a distinctive and intriguing type of American textile art. They were popular in the late nineteenth century and are experiencing a tremendous resurgence. An antique charm quilt contains an exceptional array of the textiles available when the quilt was made. As a result, they are popular as collectibles today.

The second step on our journey involved challenge quilts. Many kinds of challenges have been introduced in recent years. Some are sponsored by fabric manufacturers, and they attract quilters from all over the world. Some are proposed by local quilt groups and have fewer participants. Our challenge included only two quilters from the same city (we started small). With the publication of this book, we hope to entice other quilters to take up the Ultimate Challenge.

Challenges usually require the use of a specific fabric. Within the confines of a few rules, quilters are challenged to create quilts that include this fabric. We have seen the results of some of these fabric challenges at quilt exhibits, and they are breathtaking.

We have also heard of, and participated in, a variety of other types of challenges. Some of these required the use of specific designs, shapes, themes, or sizes. They also included progressive work from one quilter to another, or collaborative work, where two or more quilters work together to produce the desired result. Whatever the type of challenge, we have seen quilters expand their horizons by participating in these unique activities.

The third step down the Ultimate Challenge path was working in a series. This involves choosing an idea—a theme, design, or technique—then exploring it in depth by making several quilts based on the idea. For example, some quilters have made series of quilts using their favorite technique. Colorwashes, bargellos, photo transfers, and fabric paints are all excellent techniques that could be examined within a series. Our challenge involved completing a number of small quilts until a specific amount of fabric was used up. This pushed both of us to work in a series—something we had not tried before.

We wrote this book to share our idea with you and to encourage you to try some new things. We hope you find our quilts inspiring. Maybe they will spur you on to try a quilt that you've had in mind for quite some time. They might offer a new twist on an old idea, or send your mind off to explore a unique design. Whatever direction our quilts take you, we hope it will be one you have never explored before.

This book is not meant to be an instructional text for the beginner. There are many wonderful books on the market that fill that need. Our goal is to inspire every quilter, regardless of skill level, to try something new. Sometimes when we challenge ourselves, we reach new and unexpected heights. It is by the very act of exploring and stretching that we achieve. In the words of Ralph Waldo Emerson:

Unless you try to do something beyond what you have already mastered, you will never grow.

We invite you to accept the Ultimate Challenge and hope you enjoy it as much as we did. If you accept the Ultimate Challenge, you will grow as a quilter. You may explore new techniques to get the results you want. You may change the way you look at color. You may learn to like working on a small scale. You may start designing your own quilts. You may make a new friend. Who knows where the Ultimate Challenge might lead? We can't predict your destination, but we *can* guarantee the trip will be an adventure.

— *Cathy and Tammy*

•CHARM QUILTS•

Historically, quilters collected fabrics for charm quilts from family and friends. Some quilters were known to beg for fabrics from neighbors and acquaintances. As a result, charm quilts were also referred to as beggar's quilts.

There is much folklore that surrounds charm quilts. Some stories relay that each charm quilt was supposed to contain 999 pieces. Once the 999th piece was stitched into the top, the young quilter would meet her one true love. By the time the charm quilt was hand quilted, she would be ready for the wedding and would use the quilt on her wedding night. Another tale contends that if a couple "slept" under a charm quilt, they would have good luck conceiving a child. It has also been told that one duplicate fabric was deliberately placed in some charm quilts to keep a sick child occupied during his or her convalescence. The child could spend hours searching for the two like patches.

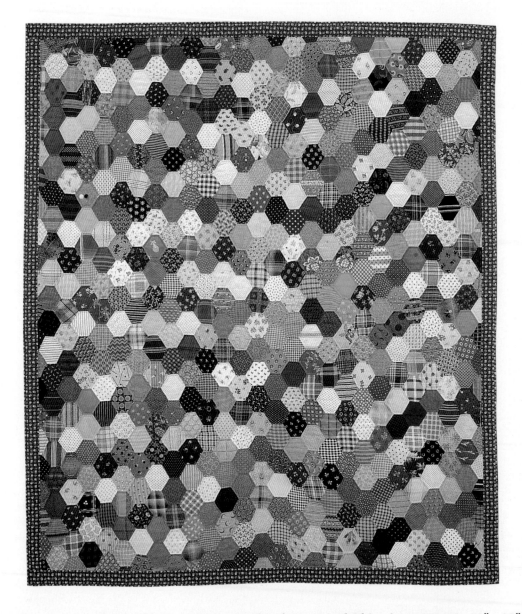

Antique charm quilt pieced by an unknown quilter from central Ohio, circa 1860–80, 72" x 85"
Quilted by Catherine L. McIntee, January, 1995, Troy, Michigan.
This charm quilt contains a delightful array of nineteenth-century fabrics,
including many conversation prints.

The Idea

The idea is quite simple. We used a set of gradated fabrics to make a master set of fabric squares. We chose a series of designs and blocks that contained the exact number of fabrics in our master set. We challenged ourselves to make a series of small quilts. Each of the quilts would contain pieces cut from each fabric in our master set. Then, for the Ultimate Challenge, we tried to make as many quilts as possible. It's really not as hard as it sounds.

The first part of the Ultimate Challenge involves selecting fabric for a palette. Each fabric must be a different print. These fabrics are then gradated by color and value. Look at the sample palette below. It contains sixty-four different gradated fabrics.

Next, fabric squares are prepared. One square is cut—for example, 4" x 4"—from each fabric in the palette. These squares are called a master set.

For each quilt in the series, an *identical portion* is cut from each fabric square in the master set. For example, to make a Nine Patch quilt, you might cut a 1" square from each fabric in your master set, then combine the squares with other fabrics to make blocks. If you want to make a Rail Fence for your second quilt, you might cut a 1" x 2" rectangle from each fabric square in your master set.

Each successive quilt requires another portion of the fabric in the master set. The diagram at right illustrates how pieces could be cut from a master set of 4" squares to make ten little quilts. Each of the resulting quilts would contain the same sixty-four fabrics, as well as lots of other fabrics of your choice. The Ultimate Challenge will have been met when the fabric squares in your master set have been used up.

In case you are still confused, don't worry. We have provided a step-by-step guide in "Accepting the Ultimate Challenge" on pages 49–51.

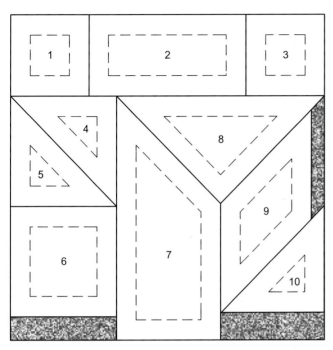

1. Nine Patch
2. Rail Fence
3. Churn Dash
4. Mini Pinwheel
5. Birds in the Air
6. Square within a Square
7. Attic Windows
8. Flying Geese
9. Clay's Choice
10. Basket

Our Experience

By now, we hope you have read the introduction and the idea chapter. We assume you've looked at the pictures. (That's the first thing we do when we get a new book.) Maybe you are wondering where in the world this idea came from. This chapter explains how two normal quilters became so engrossed in the Ultimate Challenge that it consumed our thought processes, stretched our creative talents, and pushed our technical abilities to the limit. Not to mention the effect it had on our houses, spouses, kids, and jobs. We stumbled into the Ultimate Challenge without realizing what we were getting into, but you can't use that excuse if you decide to accept the challenge.

It started rather innocently. Both of us had been collecting charm squares for several years. We had been sharing fabric squares cut from our purchases and finds in hopes of increasing the number of different fabrics in our collections. In early 1991, while pouring over a long-awaited quilt magazine, Cathy came across an advertisement for charm packets of 100 different 5" squares. The ad sparked an idea for Tammy's birthday gift, and the order for two sets was placed. When the squares arrived, Cathy put one set in her own charm stash and wrapped the second as a present for Tammy. End of story? Hardly.

A few months later, Tammy created the first quilt in what later proved to be our long and exciting quilt project. She presented Cathy, a collector of antique thimbles, with a thimble quilt as a token of friendship. "Thimbles" (page 12) contains 100 thimble shapes cut from the original 100 charm fabrics in the birthday packet. This was the spark that started the Ultimate Challenge fire, but it wasn't fanned for quite a while.

One week later, Cathy started a miniature quilt that required lots of different fabrics. She broke open her charm packet of 100 fabrics for the first time and produced "Flip Side" (page 13). It proved to be such a quick and satisfying project that her creative juices started flowing. Cathy began working on a companion piece to "Thimbles," the quilt Tammy had made for her. The new quilt would contain 100 spools of different colored thread and would be a surprise gift for Tammy.

We both produced more quilts using the charm-packet fabrics. Each successive quilt generated greater interest in how we could use the 5" squares. We experimented during this phase, using additional fabrics with our charm squares. We were off and running.

Changing Perspectives

The Ultimate Challenge changes your perspective on quilt blocks and design. The rules introduce new guidelines for choosing quilt patterns. Each quilt in our series was a different design challenge. The excitement of figuring it out was the same on the first quilt as it was on the last. Here's a story that illustrates just how this project began to affect the way we looked at quilts in a whole new light.

We were sitting together at a local quilt-guild meeting, watching a slide show. A magnificent quilt appeared on the screen. Each of us, immediately and silently, began analyzing its components to see if the design could be used for our next challenge quilt. We both figured out at the same time that it wouldn't work mathematically and shook our heads in disappointment. When we realized what had just happened, we attempted to muffle our laughter. Our attempt didn't work. The crowd around us just thought the two crazies had gone off the deep end again!

A great part about the Ultimate Challenge is that it can be as easy or difficult as you want to make it. Each pattern you choose or draft can be as simple as a Rail Fence or as complex as a Feathered Star. Our quilts range in difficulty from the simplest Nine Patch to the complexity of piecing and drafting 4" Mariner's Compass blocks with twenty points each. Some of the quilts stretched our technical abilities to the limit, or prompted us to tear our hair out. Others were sheer pleasure and went together effortlessly.

To meet the Ultimate Challenge, we employed many techniques and pieced both by hand and by machine. Several of our quilts were hand appliquéd. We machine quilted most of our pieces, but hand quilted when it was appropriate and when we felt like it. Sometimes we came up with a great design idea, but were stumped on how to execute it. These problems prompted creative solutions. Occasionally, we modified an existing technique to solve the problem. If this didn't work, we had to figure out a new way to make our ideas come to life. As a result, we folded, flipped, fused, glued, stenciled, transferred, embroidered, and stuffed our way through forty quilts. "Tips and Techniques" (pages 51–58) contains directions for some of the more unusual solutions to our technical problems.

Working as a Team

Our collaboration on "Spools for a Friend" (page 14) was the start of our development as a team. Cathy was having a problem with the border treatment. Without letting Tammy know the quilt was for her, Cathy asked for her opinion on the border. This turned out to be the first of many times one of us sought the opinion of the other. We bounced ideas off one another and relied on each other's judgment. We trusted each other enough to ask for alternate ideas, but rejected suggestions without fear of repercussion. We found that solutions to technical problems were only a phone call away. This feeling of partnership turned out to be the most wonderful side effect of the entire challenge.

We discovered we work much better together than we do separately. We produce better individual results. We come up with more interesting ideas or trash an idea we knew wasn't working anyway. We have more fabric to choose from because we share that, too, when the need arises. We learned to be more honest with each other. Unfortunately, this type of collaboration doesn't always work for all quilters. Learning to work as a team takes time. There must be an underlying respect for the talent, work ethic, creativity, feelings, and intelligence of the other quilter. If you have a quilting partner and want to grow as quilters together, take up the Ultimate Challenge. If you really want to see how strong your partnership is, try writing a book together!

Defining Your Challenge

While we were fortunate enough to work as partners, the Ultimate Challenge can be accepted by one quilter or can be picked up by an entire guild. A single quilter living on an isolated farm can follow the challenge guidelines and embark on a solo journey. If, however, you can find a soul mate who is as crazy about quilting as you are, the benefits will multiply. Your common interest will expand and your friendship will grow.

We made up the rules of our challenge as we went along. That was as much fun as any other part of the process. No one else could tell us what we should or shouldn't do. As a result, neither one of us felt too bad about bending those rules as needed.

Our quilts can be categorized as beginner, intermediate, advanced, or insane. As you look at our finished quilts, decide for yourself what category you might put them in. Then look to them for inspiration, and make a quilt that fits your level of experience. Push yourself to try something new. Let our experience charge you up. We dare you to accept the Ultimate Challenge.

Gallery of Quilts

Thimbles *by Tammy L. Porath* • *18" x 22"*
October 13 to October 14, 1991 • *Machine pieced, machine quilted*

Tammy made this first quilt in the Ultimate
Challenge series as a surprise birthday gift
for Cathy. It clearly illustrates the idea of using 100 charm units cut from a master set.

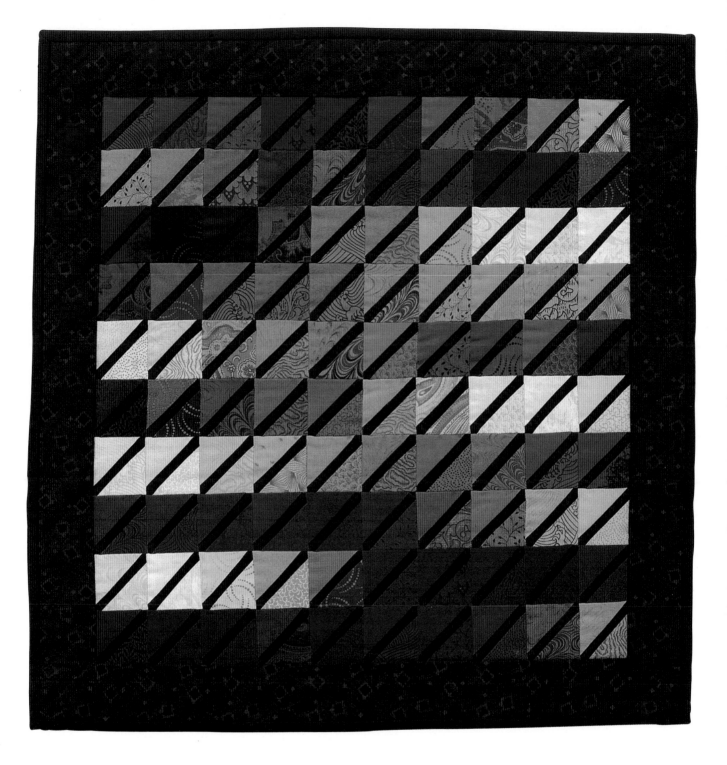

Flip Side by *Catherine L. McIntee* • *17" x 18"*   pg 61
October 19 to October 24, 1991 • *Machine pieced, hand quilted*

This first quilt in Cathy's series uses both the right and wrong side of each of the 100 fabrics in her master set. Hence the title, "Flip Side." Hand quilting through all the seam allowances prompted Cathy to machine quilt many of her other Ultimate Challenge quilts.

Spools for a Friend *by Catherine L. McIntee* • *20½" x 24"*
January 11 to January 20, 1992 • *Machine pieced, folded miters, machine quilted*

This piece was made in response to Tammy's "Thimbles" quilt and as a gift for her. The body of each spool contains one of the 100 fabrics in Cathy's master set. She used a folding technique to form the spool tops and bottoms to avoid mitering four hundred ¼" corners. Refer to "Tips and Techniques" on page 53 to learn this great little mitering method.

Fanatic *by Tammy L. Porath* • *22½" x 38"* pg 67
February 8 to April 5, 1992 • *Machine pieced, hand appliquéd, hand quilted*

After receiving "Spools for a Friend" from Cathy, Tammy was inspired to work on another charm design. This quilt's unusual setting is the result of discovering, too late, that twenty blocks can't be set on point evenly. The pieced border was designed to use background fabrics left over from making the Grandmother's Fan blocks.

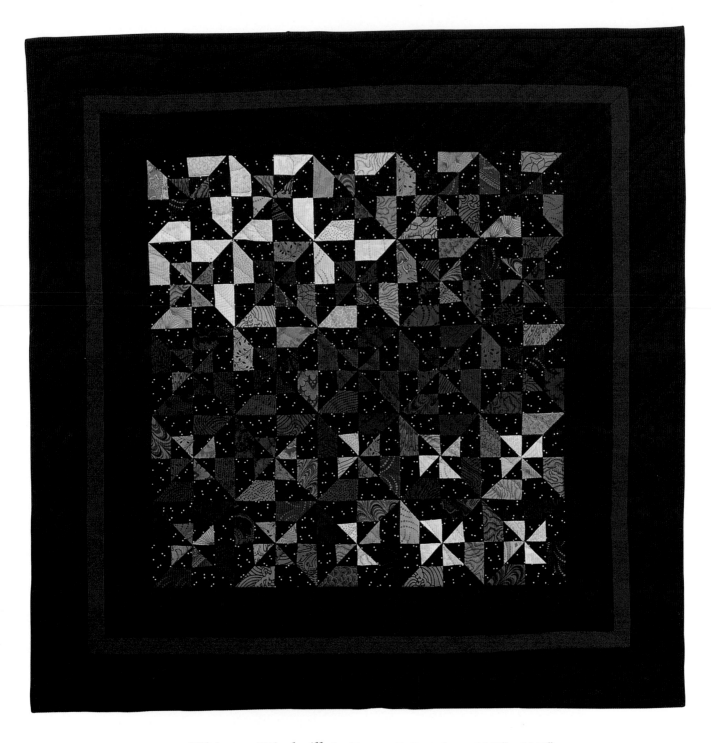

Tilting at Windmills *by Tammy L. Porath* • *19¼" x 19¼"*
February 15 to September 23, 1992 • *Machine pieced, machine quilted*

Each charm fabric appears twice in this quilt. Tammy made the blocks in pairs, alternating the light and dark values in each pair.

A productive period began with the creation of this top; several challenge tops followed in rapid succession.

Cut Your Losses by Tammy L. Porath • 10½" x 26"
February 20 to April 8, 1992 • Machine pieced, machine quilted

Here is a good example of how small errors in piecing can add up fast. Tammy pieced the rows of this quilt from the bottom toward the top. Each row crept up about 3/32" without being noticed. By the time all the rows were sewn together, the right side was ¾" higher than the left. After several attempts to correct the problem, Tammy decided to go with the flow and "cut her losses."

Crown of Thorns *by Catherine L. McIntee* • *17" x 17"* ~~pg 71~~
February 22 to March 1, 1992 • *Machine pieced, hand and machine quilted*

Made before Cathy discovered paper piecing, this quilt was an exercise that demanded extreme accuracy. Much to her delight, it came out as flat as a pancake! Choosing a wide variety of fabrics was a real challenge and an absolute joy.

***Milky Way** by Tammy L. Porath • 16½" x 16½"* pg 66
February 22 to April 7, 1992 • Machine pieced, machine quilted

Tammy used a set of hand-dyed gray fabrics to their best advantage in this piece. A simple block design and an on-point setting produced just the right look. In-the-ditch stitches outline each block, and quilted stars in the border repeat the piecing motif.

Facets by Tammy L. Porath • *13½" x 13½"*
February 24 to April 7, 1992 • *Machine pieced, machine quilted*

After piecing "Milky Way," Tammy had 100 leftover half-square triangle units. Quilters never let anything go to waste, so she spent five or six hours twisting and turning those little units to get an interesting design. The hand-dyed gray fabrics create the illusion of a three-dimensional border.

Snapdragons by *Tammy L. Porath* • *37" x 37½"* yeq 69
February 26, 1992 to May 25, 1993 • *Machine pieced, hand appliquéd, machine quilted*

The center of this quilt has relatively simple piecing and appliqué. Tammy decided to enhance the center design with a vine-and-bud border, which used all 100 charm fabrics.

Implementing this idea meant appliquéing 300 more pieces! The three-dimensional folded bud in the border was the most challenging part of the quilt.

Look Ma, No Seam Allowances *by Catherine L. McIntee* • *9" x 15"*
February 27, 1992 • *Spatula applied, machine overstitched, machine quilted*

Perhaps the most fun and definitely the fastest of the quilts Cathy made, this little treasure occurred spontaneously. While trimming away the excess seam allowances for "Crown of Thorns," the scraps fell in a semi-grouped color arrangement that was too wonderful to sweep into the wastebasket. Two kitchen spatulas were used to lift the fallen scraps and carefully place them on the base fabric. Refer to pages 53–54 to create a spontaneous treasure of your own.

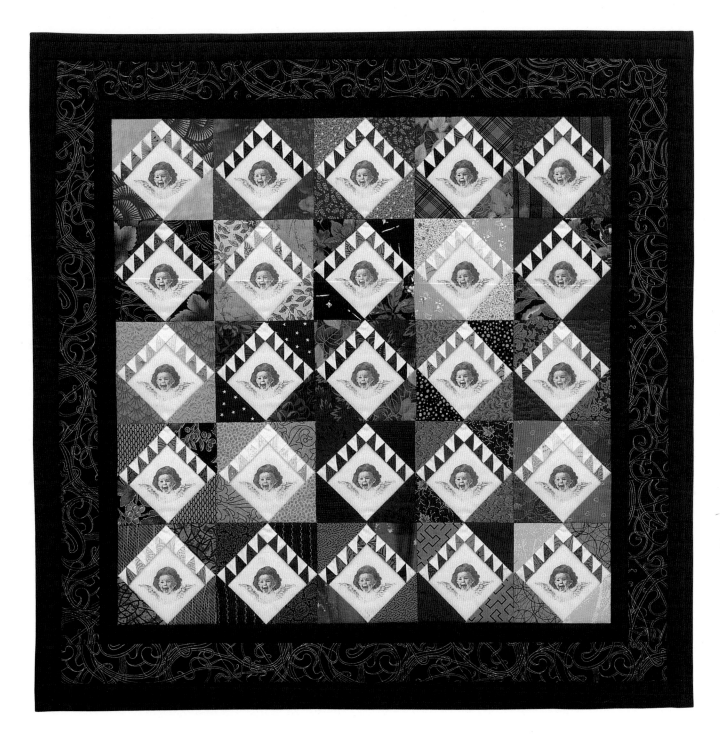

My Angel Baby *by Catherine L. McIntee* • *25" x 25"*

February 28 to March 9, 1992 • *Machine pieced, photo-transferred images, machine quilted*

The inspiration for this piece came from a birthday card sent to Cathy's youngest daughter. A photo of Colleen's face had been photocopied, cut out, colored, and pasted into a cherub angel drawing. The image on the card was the perfect thing to fill the space in the block design. Colleen is especially proud of her starring role in this quilt.

***Mama's Quilting II** by Catherine L. McIntee • 24" x 19"*
March 2 to April 11, 1992 • Hand appliquéd, machine pieced, machine quilted

When Cathy saw this delightful pattern by Bunny Publications, she immediately knew what her next challenge would be. Could all 100 fabrics from a master set be included in the quilt the women were working on?

Not one to shy away from a challenge, Cathy set to work mapping out ¼" pieces into the available quilt space. The design was slightly modified to include all 100 pieces.

***Chinese Coins** by Tammy L. Porath* • *10¼" x 15½"*
March 18 to April 8, 1992 • Machine pieced, hand beaded, hand and machine quilted

By the time this quilt was made, the idea for the Ultimate Challenge was fully developed. Even the littlest pieces weren't wasted. Tammy had 100 rectangles that were too small to work into a block, so she sewed them into rows, using a ⅛"-wide seam allowance. Bugle beads were added during the quilting process to jazz up the quilt.

Grandmother's Choice *by Tammy L. Porath* • *23½" x 27"* fg 65
March 19, 1992 to May 21, 1993 • *Machine pieced, machine quilted*

After making several contemporary designs, Tammy wanted to try something traditional. Multiple background fabrics provide a wide variety of wonderful textures on the surface of this quilt. The sashing grid also creates the illusion of depth.

Flocks of Geese by Catherine L. McIntee • *15" x 15"*   pg. 62
March 21 to March 22, 1992 • *Machine pieced, machine quilted*

This weekend special was both quick and fun. The center section went together easily, but Cathy's original choice for the border fabric just didn't do the trick. After a quick telephone call, Cathy hopped in the car to head to Tammy's house for a consultation. Tammy pulled out just the right black fabric from her stash, and new borders were cut. A perfect solution!

Peaks and Valleys by *Catherine L. McIntee* • *18" x 16"* pg 64
March 28 to March 31, 1992 • *Machine pieced, machine quilted*

A cross between two classic patterns—Delectable Mountains and Anvils—produced this arrangement. The colors were divided equally between each of the five rows, and the fabric selections worked beautifully. An all-time favorite fabric was used in the border to tie everything together. Cathy is especially proud of this piece.

Fusion *by Tammy L. Porath* • *10" x 11½"*
March 28 to March 31, 1992 • *Fused, machine pieced, machine quilted*

During this challenge, extreme measures were sometimes used to avoid wasting anything. A multitude of tiny charm pieces were fused to the background fabric individually. Peeling paper backings, positioning scraps, and fusing them took much longer than Tammy had anticipated. The organza overlay stabilized the fused pieces, and the silver trim added spark.

Time for Everything—A Quilter's Wish by Tammy L. Porath • 12¾" x 14"
April 1 to April 3, 1992 • Machine pieced, machine quilted

Since this quilt was based on a simple block, Tammy wanted to do something special with the background. In the finished quilt, a set of hand-dyed fabrics blend beautifully with the charm palette. As unlikely as it seems, a ¼-yard piece of Madras plaid adds the perfect touch for a final border.

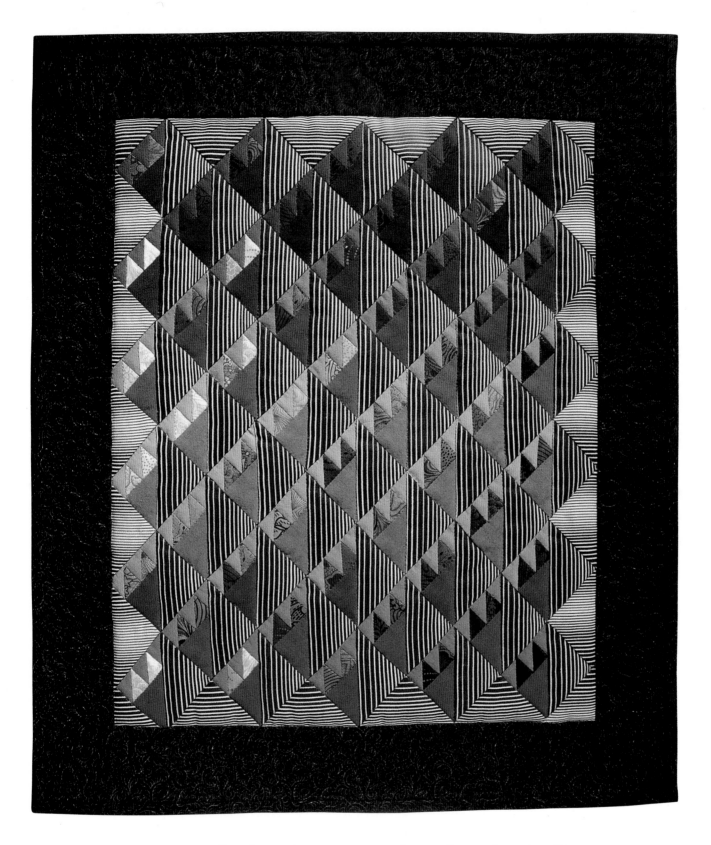

***Southpaw** by Tammy L. Porath* • *15" x 17½"* fig 63
April 6 to April 8, 1992 • *Machine pieced, machine quilted*

Since discovering that fifty blocks can be set on point evenly, Tammy started looking for blocks that had two charm units. She found the Rosebud block and liked the idea of using only one quarter of it as a block. The black stripe and a set of hand-dyed fabrics were chosen. A plain border was added to contrast with the pieced center.

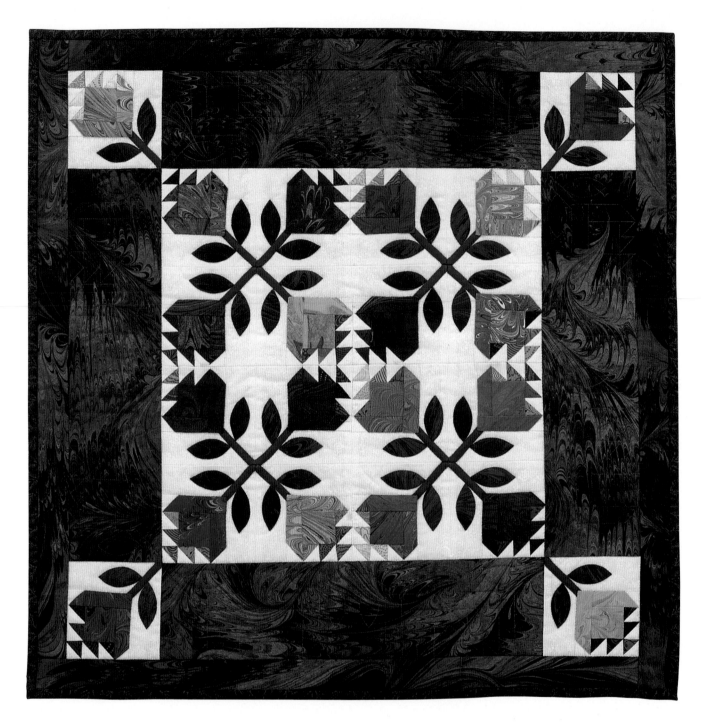

What "Marbelous" Tulips by Catherine L. McIntee • *20" x 20"* pg 70
April 12 to April 26, 1992 • *Machine pieced, stuffed, hand appliquéd, machine quilted*

Having collected a large assortment of Japanese marbled cottons, this quilt was just the excuse Cathy needed to acquire even more!

Several "marbelous" Japanese fabrics form the body of each tulip, and the 100 charm fabrics can be found in the tulip points.

Running in Circles *by Catherine L. McIntee* • *15" in diameter*
April 26 to May 2, 1992 • *Glued, fused, machine appliquéd, hand quilted*

An L-shaped shred, left over from a previous cut, defied the trash and prompted this circular quilt. Keeping the miniature pieces in order and intact was the toughest part of constructing this piece. A pin, a fabric gluestick, and lots of patience made it possible. Hand quilting the feather wreath while watching the Kentucky Derby on television triggered the name for this quilt.

The Tree of One Hundred Blossoms *by Tammy L. Porath* • *27" x 26½"*

January 26 to May 18, 1993 • *Stenciled, hand appliquéd and beaded, machine pieced, hand and machine quilted*

Here is another example of scraps used to extremes! Tammy's only idea for using this scrap was a type of Yo-yo flower. After deciding on a flowering tree design, she stenciled the tree trunk, branches, and grass on the background sky fabric. Each flower was then gathered, appliquéd, and beaded.

Tubes by Catherine L. McIntee • *13" x 15"*

February 13 to February 20, 1993 • *Machine pieced, stuffed, hand appliquéd, machine quilted*

Ever tried to insert a cotton piping cord through a 10-foot tube of fabric with 100 seam allowances inside? If not, don't. This problem prompted Cathy to create the Pieced and Stuffed Tubes technique described on pages 56–57. She originally envisioned a tube that would gracefully drape over the surface of a base fabric, like a pile of spaghetti.

Unfortunately, the tube was so stiff you could have pole vaulted with it! As a result, the tube was cut into ten 12" sections, and each section was appliquéd to the base. Machine stitching secured the top and bottom edges of the tubes. It is a much different quilt than originally planned, but just as exciting.

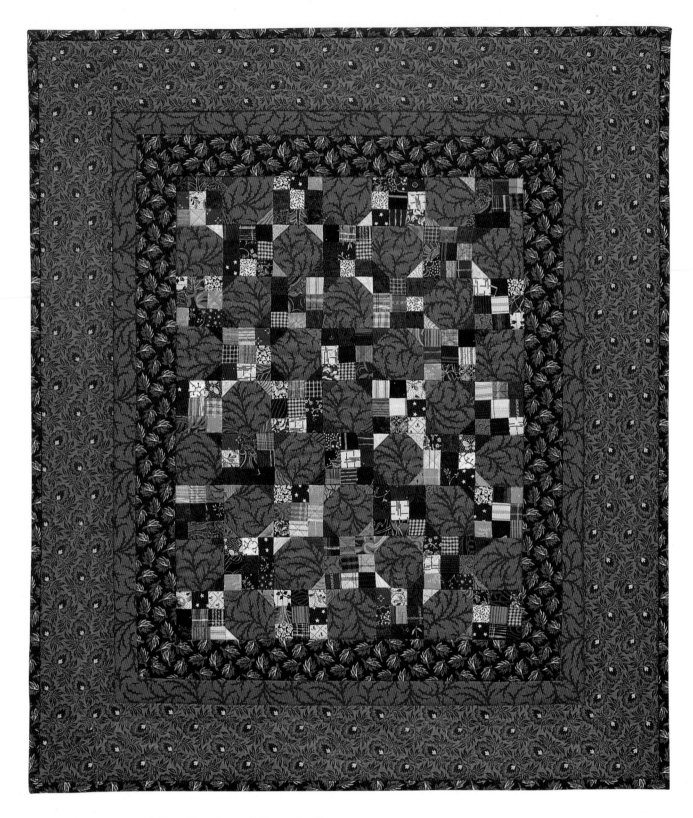

Nine Patch and Snowball *by Catherine L. McIntee* • *18" x 21"*
May 6 to May 10, 1993 • *Machine pieced, machine quilted*

A consuming interest in quilts from the late nineteenth century inspired this quilt. The use of double pinks and the combination of two classic blocks demonstrates how wonderful simplicity can be.

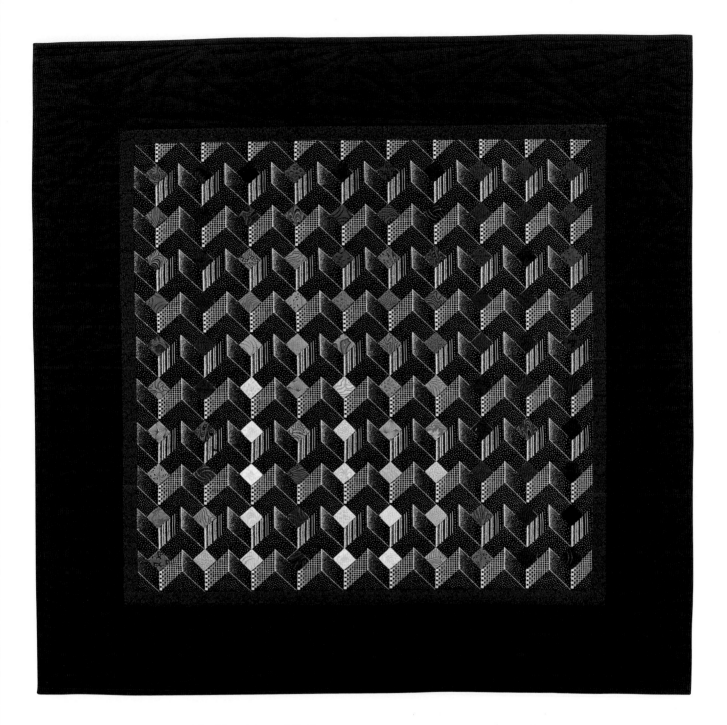

Feeling Boxed In? *by Catherine L. McIntee* • *32" x 31"*
August 12 to August 24, 1993 • *Hand appliquéd, machine pieced, hand quilted*

The base fabric in this quilt was a gift Tammy gave to Cathy. Inspiration hit, and Cathy appliquéd 100 squares, each ¾", to add sparks of color to the grid. A great piece of fabric, a simple idea, some appliqué skill, and lots of patience produced this little gem.

Data's Universe *by Tammy L. Porath* • *24" x 24"*
October 15, 1993 to June 1, 1994 • *Paper pieced, hand appliquéd, machine quilted*

Since cutting the fan blades for "Fanatic," Tammy had been trying to decide what to do with a long, skinny leftover scrap. After a lot of drafting, she came up with a Mariner's Compass pattern. Paper-piecing techniques made stitching the blocks possible. A planet design fabric was used for the background and border. Tammy is an avid *Star Trek: The Next Generation* fan, and while working on this top, the title "Data's Universe" kept popping into her head.

Twisted Rope by Catherine L. McIntee • 13½" x 13½"
October 16 to October 17, 1993 • Machine pieced, machine quilted

What Cathy thought was to be her final quilt in the Ultimate Challenge languished for months as a scribbled design in her memo book. One last push on a rainy weekend made this design a reality. It was with some relief, admittedly, that the final stitches were put into the binding on this, the last of Cathy's series… or so she thought.

Finally by Catherine L. McIntee • *49" x 58"*   pg 68

June 11 to October 22, 1994 • Paper pieced, fused, machine quilted

A closer look at Cathy's master diagram revealed yet another 1¼" unused square of fabric. The excitement of completing the one last step to meet the Ultimate Challenge set in. After choosing the Christmas Cactus Variation block, a ramble through her scrap drawer produced many of the eighty other fabrics needed for the quilt. A marvelous floral fabric was cut up, arranged, fused, and appliquéd to produce the twelve different flower clusters in the alternate squares.

***Cuckoo Clock** by Tammy L. Porath • 26½" x 34"*
July 1 to October 7, 1994 • Paper pieced, machine appliquéd, machine quilted

A wonderful little paper-pieced bird was the original inspiration for this quilt. Tammy thought about putting these cute birds into houses, nests, or trees, but finally decided on the cuckoo clock. The bird patterns, clock face, and overall quilt layout were drafted and printed on a computer. The clock face was then traced onto fabric using a light box and permanent fabric markers.

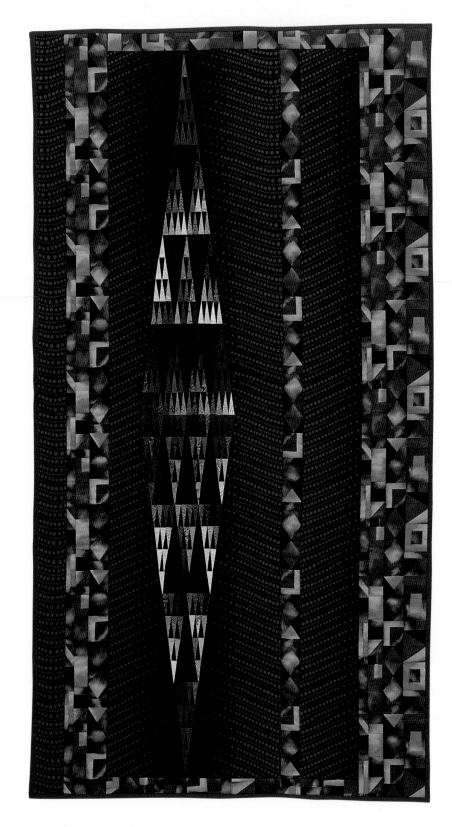

Diamonds Are Forever *by Tammy L. Porath* • *23" x 44"*
October 10 to October 13, 1994 • *Fused, machine pieced, machine quilted*

Two skinny scraps called for Tammy's attention and were turned into this unusual quilt. Her technique for fusing extremely small pieces of fabric was used to complete the diamond in the center. (This technique is described on page 52.) The quilt was finished with simple borders and outline quilting.

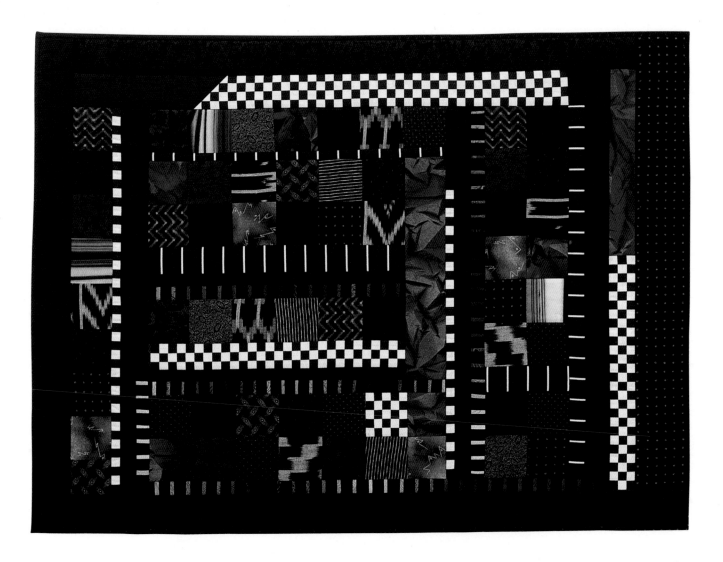

One Dark and Stormy Night *by Catherine L. McIntee • 38" x 28"*
October 15 to October 21, 1994 • Machine pieced, machine quilted

The last scrap in Cathy's master set seemed almost impossible to use. Weeks went by without an idea, and a deadline was approaching. This wonderfully modern quilt was completely unplanned and came together mostly during one day of spontaneous design flurry. A marked contrast to the cheerful flowers of "Finally," this piece triggers thoughts of a dark and mysterious night.

Lest You Think We Made No Mistakes

You may have marveled at the fact that we were able to create these wonderful quilts, using every little bit of our master set of squares without making any mistakes. Wrong. We make lots of mistakes, but are just getting better at covering them up.

We made cutting mistakes, poor design decisions, unappealing fabric choices, and pieces we thought were just not so hot when they were finished. Not being ones to give up, we would just start over. Sometimes the new pieces were much better than if we hadn't made the error in the first place. Just for the fun of it, we thought you would enjoy seeing some of our mistakes.

If you make a mistake, don't look back. Pick yourself up, dust yourself off, and start over again. After all, we are just human beings who can mis-cut, mis-measure, mis-stitch, and occasionally make bad color choices. That's the good thing about quilting—unlike medicine, no one dies from your mistakes. Learn what you can, and try again. Most importantly, don't run yourself down if you do take a mis-step. Remember, we do this for pleasure. Enjoy!

Accepting the Ultimate Challenge

Follow these easy guidelines, and you'll be well on your way to meeting the Ultimate Challenge. Have fun.

Prepare

1. Look at the photos in this book. (We all do that first anyway.)
2. Read "The Idea" (page 6) to find out where you are going.
3. Read through the instructions in this chapter before getting started to avoid making any really bad mistakes.
4. Locate at least one other quilter who is bored with what she is presently doing, or who doesn't have enough unfinished projects already. Convince your fellow quilter(s) to accept the Ultimate Challenge, using any reasonable or unreasonable arguments. (If you can't find another quilter to join you in this adventure, proceed to step 5. You'll still have a ball.)

Create Your Master Set

5. Decide on the number of different fabrics to include in your master set. A master set is a collection of squares cut from a gradated fabric palette. We used 100 different fabrics in our master set because that was the number in our original charm packets. Select a number that is evenly divisible by as many other numbers as possible. This will broaden your design choices later on. Below is a list of possible numbers and their divisors. Notice that 60, 96, and 120 present the most options, making them ideal choices.

    60 is divisible by 1, 2, 3, 4, 5, 6, 10, 12, 15
    64 is divisible by 1, 2, 4, 8, 16
    96 is divisible by 1, 2, 3, 4, 6, 8, 12, 16
    100 is divisible by 1, 2, 4, 5, 10
    120 is divisible by 1, 2, 3, 4, 5, 6, 8, 10, 12, 15

6. Choose your fabrics. Assemble fabrics that can be color gradated, and include every major color in the spectrum. Small-scale prints or tone-on-tone fabrics that look solid from a distance are good choices. You could even use all solids. Large-scale designs, multicolor fabrics, and busy prints do not work well for this project.
7. Cut one square of the same size from each different fabric. A 5" square worked well for us, but you may want to try a larger square if you're not crazy about

working with small pieces or miniatures. You have now assembled your master set of fabric squares.

NOTE:

If you convinced a friend(s) to join you in tackling the Ultimate Challenge, you both may want to begin with identical master sets. If so, cut two squares at the same time from each fabric you have chosen. It's easier and faster than doing it separately. You will be amazed to see the different results that stem from identical master sets.

·TIP·

Here are a few ways to collect a large assortment of charm squares:

- Purchase charm squares from a quilters' catalog. To ensure recovery from mistakes, we each ordered an extra set of identical charm squares as a back-up. When we made a cutting mistake or produced quilts that didn't work for one reason or another, those extra sets came in handy. The mistake pieces were recut from the spare charm set, and we were able to try again.
- Join a fabric club. They usually send out collections of charm squares on a monthly basis.
- Place an ad in a quilt magazine. Charm-exchange listings are usually free of charge.
- Answer charm-exchange advertisements in quilt magazines. This is quicker than placing an ad, but you will get fewer squares. Respond to advertisements from recent back issues as well.
- If you belong to a quilt guild or group, volunteer to organize a charm-square swap. This is a popular activity and lots of fun.
- Get together with other quilters who wish to embark on the Ultimate Challenge. Ask a quilt shop to prepare charm packets for your group.

---

8. Gradate your master set. Look at the sample palette on page 6 if you need help getting started. First, group the squares by color, then put them in order from lightest to darkest. This will help you determine if you have included fabrics from the entire color spectrum and if you have included a full range of values. If necessary, make corrections to your master set before proceeding.

Search for Ideas

9. Search for design ideas or block patterns that could accommodate the exact number of fabrics in your master set. These can be traditional or original designs. Your choices must contain a certain number of units, which are the pieces in a design that are the same shape and size.

   For example, let's say your master set contains 60 fabrics. Any pattern that contains 1, 2, 3, 4, 5, 6, 10, 12, or 15 units would work because 60 is evenly divisible by these numbers. The Corn and Beans block shown below illustrates two options for placing fabrics from your master set. In the first diagram, 12 different charm fabrics are placed in each block. Using this placement option, you would produce 5 blocks. In the second illustration, 6 charm fabrics are placed in each block. You could make 10 blocks using this placement option. If you made the Corn and Beans block, but had 120 fabrics in your master set, you would end up with more blocks. Additional blocks increase the layout possibilities for your quilt.

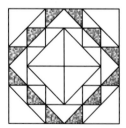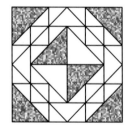

Corn and Beans

   Patterns containing 7, 8, or 9 units would not work with a master set of 60 fabrics because 60 is not evenly divisible by these numbers. As you can see, 60 is a good number for your master set because it provides so many options. Other magic numbers are 96 and 120.

   "Block Ideas" (pages 73–75) contains 38 block patterns illustrating possible charm-fabric placements.

10. Select other fabrics from your stash to use in your quilt in addition to the fabrics from your master set. In this challenge there is no limit to the additional fabrics you can use. As you can see in our quilts, we often used neutrals, black, and white, and also experimented with lots of scraps and a variety of color schemes.

11. Choose or design a layout for your quilt. Use your imagination and don't confine yourself to traditional settings. We incorporated many different settings and quilt shapes in our series. If your design lends itself to an unusual shape, go for it. There is no rule that says a quilt must be a square or a rectangle.

Ready, Set, Sew!

12. Work on a quilt top when the inspiration hits you. You can always quilt it later. As you can tell by looking at the start and finish dates in the gallery, Tammy is comfortable with a flexible schedule. Cathy, however, tends to complete one quilt before proceeding to the next. Do whatever makes you comfortable.

13. Quilt the finished pieces. Many of our small tops were much easier to quilt by machine due to the number of seam allowances. We hand quilted where we could and when we wanted.

Finish Up

14. Think of neat names for your quilts. If you chose a classic pattern, you could use the traditional pattern name. If you designed something yourself or created a variation of a classic pattern, then give it an original name. You can even use subtitles if you have more than one idea for a name.

   Making a quilt is a lot like having a baby. Between us, we have six kids and they all have names. Who doesn't give their child a name? So why not name your quilts?

15. Sign and date your quilts. If you are working in a series, include the sequence number on the label. Don't forget your city and state. It is important to document your quilts. Quilt historians of the future will thank you. Many of us own antique quilts and have no idea who made them, when they were made, or where the maker lived. You are the artist and you should be proud of your work. Don't let the term "anonymous quilter" apply to you.

Use permanent-ink markers to write on labels. Press freezer paper to the back of the label to stabilize the fabric while you write. The label can be as simple or elaborate as you wish. There are books available that include fancy borders and floral decorations for embellishing quilt labels. Use excess binding to put a matching border around the label before attaching it to the back of your quilt.

16. Photograph your quilts. If you don't own a camera, borrow one. The cost of film and developing is minuscule compared to the time spent making your quilt.

17. Show your quilts to other people. Start with family and friends if you're hesitant. Enter your quilts in local shows. If you're unsure about having your quilts judged, submit them for exhibit only. Share your work with others so they can be inspired by your success.

18. Continue working on your series until you have used all the fabric in your master set of squares. Look again at the sample diagram on page 7. You can see how careful placement and efficient cutting leaves little waste. This is not the place to use your rotary cutter!

Summary

Here is a brief recap of the steps required to accept the Ultimate Challenge.

1. Read through this book so you'll understand what's in store for you.

2. Assemble a master set of squares, gradating by color and value.

3. Choose a quilt pattern that incorporates the exact number of fabrics in your master set. Select other fabrics to combine with the pieces from your master set.

4. Cut the pattern pieces from your master set and from additional fabrics. Piece or appliqué your quilt top. Machine or hand quilt it.

5. Name, label, and bind your quilt, then photograph it. Continue making quilts, cutting pieces from your master set until it is gone.

Congratulations! You have picked up the gauntlet and accepted the Ultimate Challenge. Enjoy each moment along the way. The more you play, experiment, work, and try, the happier you will be with the results.

Tips and Techniques

While attempting to meet the Ultimate Challenge, we used many different techniques. Some of them are a little unusual or were developed out of necessity. Even though there are many wonderful instructional texts that explore some of these techniques in greater detail, we want to share a few of the unusual ones. We hope our ingenuity inspires you to believe that "where there's a will, there's a way."

Colorized Photo Transfer

We have seen many wonderful quilts that feature photo images transferred to fabric. There are different ways to accomplish this, but most methods use black-and-white photocopy machines. Our technique adds a bit of color without using more expensive color photocopies.

1. Make several black-and-white photocopies of the design or photo you wish to transfer to fabric. The higher the quality of the photocopy, the crisper your transfer image will be.

2. Use colored pencils directly on the photocopy to lightly shade the areas you wish to highlight. Pink cheeks, red lips, blue eyes, and blond hair seemed just right for the cherubs in "My Angel Baby" (page 23). Berol Prismacolor® pencils work well.

3. Transfer the image to fabric with photo-transfer medium, which is available in most craft stores.

   a. Spread a thick coat of the transfer medium on the photocopy, using your fingers or a brush.

   b. *Immediately* place the wet transfer face down on the right side of the fabric. Carefully smooth out any air bubbles. Allow this fabric/paper sandwich to thoroughly dry for at least 24 hours. The transfer medium absorbs the carbon from the photocopy while it is drying. The image will be reversed. This is inconsequential in most cases, but is important if your design includes words or numbers.

   c. Soak the fabric/paper sandwich in warm water until the paper becomes mushy.

   d. Rub the paper off with your fingers or a soft brush. Fingertips are less likely to rub off the image.

   e. Dry the fabric flat. If paper fibers remain on the surface of the photo image, repeat the soaking and rubbing process, then re-dry. Do not touch the surface of the transfer with a hot iron or it will melt the transfer.

Embellishments

Simple glass beads, buttons, brass charms, and other embellishments liven up designs. The beading on "Chinese Coins" (page 25) adds sparkle to an otherwise dark quilt. The following methods work best on quilts that won't be handled much. If you know your quilt will be laundered, embellishments may not be advisable.

- Add beads during the hand-quilting process. Quilt as usual, until you reach the point where a bead is needed, then slide the bead onto the needle and thread. Stitch through the bead and the quilt top again to secure it. Continue quilting.

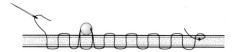

- Attach embellishments with fabric glue or hot glue, following the manufacturer's directions. This is a quick and easy way to spice up your designs. Hot glue can melt some plastics, so be sure to test it on your embellishments before applying them to your quilt.

Fabric Fusing

Paper-backed fusible web is popular for quick appliqué work. Several brands are available, and each includes complete instructions for use. This tip covers a unique twist for creating designs from tiny or odd-shaped pieces of fabric that would normally be considered scraps. This method also enables you to fuse entire miniature blocks at once.

Take a look at "Fusion" (page 31) and "Diamonds Are Forever" (page 46). The center sections of both quilts were constructed with the fabric-fusing method.

1. Cut out the shapes to be used in your design, without seam allowances, or use fabric snippets as is.
2. Place the shapes *right side up* on your ironing surface. If you are working in a block format, butt the shapes together exactly as they are positioned in your design. Don't arrange too many blocks at once because the slightest breeze will rearrange them. For ease of handling, leave at least ¼" between each block or group of shapes.

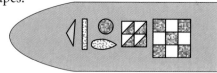

Fabric shapes right side up on ironing surface

3. Place a piece of freezer paper, waxy side down, on the arranged shapes. Press with a hot, dry iron. After the freezer paper has completely cooled, carefully peel it from your ironing surface. All the shapes are now on the freezer paper, *wrong side up*.

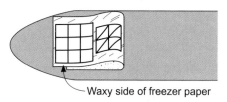

Waxy side of freezer paper

4. Place a piece of paper-backed fusible web on the waxy side of the freezer paper, covering the wrong side of the fabric shapes. Press, following the manufacturer's directions. Now you have a sandwich: freezer paper/fabric shapes/fusible web.

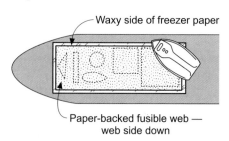

Waxy side of freezer paper

Paper-backed fusible web — web side down

5. Cut out each fabric shape or block. Do not leave any fusible web beyond the edge of the fabric.
6. Peel the freezer paper from the fabric shapes. Then carefully peel the paper backing from the fusible web. If you have fused blocks, do not tear the web between the pieces of the block. Handle the blocks gently so they won't become distorted.
7. Position each shape or block on your background fabric and fuse in place. It is not advisable to move the iron while fusing. Do not attempt to fuse more shapes than the surface of your iron can cover at one time.

Folded Half-Square Triangle Units and Miters

Most of us cringe at the thought of trying to achieve perfectly flat mitered corners. "Spools for a Friend" (page 14) posed the problem of how to easily make four hundred 45° angles. The solution was a modified folding technique.

Let's say you want to make half-square triangle units. Instead of cutting lots of small triangles and trying to feed them through the machine with the bias edges stretching like crazy, try this:

1. Cut 2 squares of fabric the size you want, including seam allowances.
2. Fold 1 square in half diagonally as shown, wrong sides together. Press the fold with a steam iron. Lay the folded triangle on top of the base square, aligning 2 sides, and pin in place.

3. Use the pinned square as you would a pieced half-square triangle unit. The fold won't be stitched down, but will appear as a folded pocket on the quilt surface.

Now that you have the general idea, let's look at other ways you can use this technique. It will come in handy for mitering small corners or anywhere a 45° angle is needed. Fold the piece that is going to be mitered *before* sewing it to another piece in your project.

- If you are working with a square, fold it diagonally from corner to corner. Press the fold with a steam iron, and pin in place. Continue piecing.
- If you are working with a rectangle, fold a short edge to a long edge. Press the fold with a steam iron and pin in place. Continue piecing.

 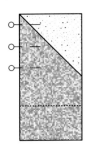

> **NOTE:**
> The fabric underneath the folded miter must be large enough to cover the exposed area. This will prevent batting from coming up through the surface of the quilt. Look at the background piece in the illustration below left. This technique does not work well with large miters, such as quilt borders, because the fold is not sewn.

"Spools for a Friend" carries the folding technique to the extreme. If you would like to imitate this quilt, sew on the tops and bottoms of the spools as a single long strip of fabric. Start and stop the stitching at each spool body. Clip the strip between each spool and fold the tail ends under at a 45° angle. Pin them in place before sewing on the background strip.

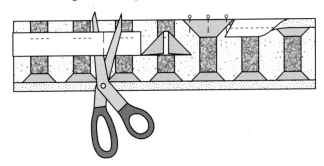

Free-Form Scraps

Did you ever try to think of what you could do with the little scraps or snippets you have trimmed from other pieces? Here is a solution. Use them as embellishments!

Simply pick up the pieces from the floor or your cutting surface and lay them on another piece of fabric. To make the pieces easier to control, apply a stabilizer or firm interfacing to the base fabric. Carefully take the whole works to your sewing machine, and randomly sew over the pieces to hold them in place. Your sewing can be planned, if you like, as long as the pieces are attached to the base when you are finished. The raw edges of the pieces will be exposed, so this technique may not work well for a quilt that will be laundered. This method was used to create "Look Ma, No Seam Allowances" (page 22).

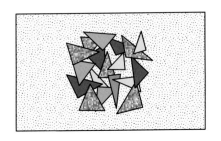

Another variation of this technique was used to construct "Running in Circles" (page 35). The snippets of fabric in this quilt were carefully arranged before being placed on the surface of the quilt.

1. Place each fabric scrap on a sandpaper-covered board in the proper order.

2. Pick up the pieces one at a time. Apply a dot of fabric glue with a pin to the wrong side of each piece.

3. Position each piece on the quilt surface. Let the glue dry thoroughly.

4. Machine quilt with invisible nylon thread or hand quilt to secure each piece. Free-form shapes will not stand up well to laundering. If you like the frayed look, try this technique with larger scraps that will only fray on the edge when washed.

NOTE:

Consider using this technique with other projects. Sprinkled scraps would look neat on a jacket as an accent, or on a multi-technique sampler quilt. Look on the floor of your sewing room for inspiration now and again. You never know what you may find!

If you want to make tiny circular scraps, stiffen your fabric with fusible interfacing. Then cut fabric circles with a hole-punch. Sew the circles to your base fabric in any way you please. As an alternative, use paper-backed fusible web: peel off the backing and press the tiny circles in place. Make sure the circles are fabric-side up when you press them, or you will end up with a polka-dotted iron faceplate.

Freezer-Paper Stencils

Traditional stenciling requires that the design be cut from stencil plastic. This is great if you are going to use the design many times. If, however, you need a stenciled shape only once, freezer-paper stenciling could be for you.

1. Trace the design onto a piece of freezer paper that is at least 1" larger all around than your design. As in traditional stenciling, cut a separate stencil for each section of the design that will be a different color. You should be able to trace most designs easily. You can use a light box or a window on a sunny day if your original is too faint.

2. Cut out the shape. Use a craft knife if there are a lot of details. Bridges between pieces aren't necessary because sections that are disconnected from the rest of the stencil during cutting can be pressed on the fabric individually. In the illustration below, the windows were cut from the freezer paper, then pressed in place on the background fabric before stenciling.

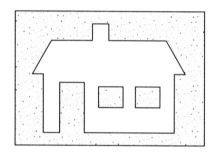

3. Press the freezer-paper stencil on the background fabric, using a hot, dry iron. Be sure to firmly seal the edges.

4. Stencil the design with fabric paint. Apply the paint by "pouncing" the brush up and down. Follow the manufacturer's directions for heat setting your project.

This method was used on "The Tree of One Hundred Blossoms" (page 36). Several colors of fabric paint were used to create the texture in the tree trunk. The freezer paper remained on the background fabric until all the colors were applied. The grass was painted freehand with a stencil brush.

Light-Box Tracings

If you have ever wanted to transfer a large, nonphotographic image to fabric, this technique could come in handy. Images smaller than 11" x 17" can easily be transferred to fabric with a special heat-transfer machine. If your image is larger than this, we've come up with another method. The process described here works well if you want to produce only one copy on fabric. Silk screening can produce multiple copies, but is too expensive for only one image transfer. Our technique can be tedious, but it can be done.

In our case, the objective was to enlarge and transfer a piece of standard-size sheet music to a 34" x 22" piece of fabric. The fabric could not be rubberized, painted, or laminated because the finished surface would be appliquéd. This ruled out using marine-sail producers and sign/flag fabricators. After much time, research, and trial and error, the solution appeared much simpler than expected. Look at "Spinning Song" (page 40) to see the finished product. You can get the same result by following these easy steps.

1. Enlarge the original image on a photocopy machine until a full-scale copy is obtained. This may require taping several sections together.

2. Stabilize your base fabric by pressing the waxy side of freezer paper to the wrong side of the fabric with a hot, dry iron. Leave the freezer paper on the base fabric until you are completely finished with this process.

3. Tape the full-scale photocopy to a light table, large window, or glass door on a sunny day. We recommend a light box because this job will take a while. Lengthy jobs strain the hands and arms if you are working on a vertical surface, such as a window.

4. Position your stabilized fabric over the image, and tape it in place with drafting or masking tape.

5. Trace the image onto the fabric with permanent-ink pens. These pens come in a wide array of widths and point styles. To outline shapes, use fine-line pens. We recommend Micron Pigma pens in .005, .01, .03, and .05 widths. For solid areas, use progressively wider pens. We like Sanford® Sharpie® Ultra Fine and Fine Point Permanent Markers. Be sure to test pens and markers on a scrap of fabric first to see if they bleed or run. Try using different fabrics to get different results. Trace as much at one time as your hands and eyes can withstand. Take breaks to relax your muscles and eyes.

6. Remove the freezer paper from the fabric when the image has been completely traced. Let the fabric set for 24 hours.

7. Using a warm, dry iron, press the base fabric to set the inks.

Paper Piecing

Paper piecing, a revival of traditional foundation piecing, is a popular technique. It allows quilters to piece small designs accurately. "Data's Universe" (page 42) would not have been possible without this technique. There are books, miniature-block kits, and many paper-piecing patterns available in quilt shops. They contain complete instructions on paper piecing. Here are a few extra hints.

- Use a photocopy machine to produce multiple paper foundations. Always check the copies against the original for accuracy.

- Don't forget that the final design will be a mirror image of the paper pattern. If it is important that the design is oriented in a certain way, reverse the pattern before photocopying. An easy way to reverse an image is to photocopy the design onto a sheet of clear acetate or overhead transparency. Flip the transparency over and photocopy it onto paper. The design is now reversed!

- Choose a block or design that has no set-in corners. All piecing must be done in straight lines. Redraft a block if necessary. Dividing a block into two or more sections can sometimes eliminate set-in corners.

- Leave the paper on each section of the design until all sections are pieced. This stabilizes bias edges and keeps the sections accurately aligned.

- With paper piecing, you don't have to be very accurate about the size of the fabric piece you are adding. It only has to be big enough to cover the intended area. Trim the seam allowances after stitching each seam to reduce bulk. Your work will also lie much flatter if you press each piece as you sew.

- Use a small stitch length (18 to 20 stitches per inch) to make paper removal easier.

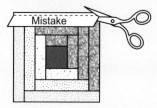
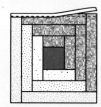
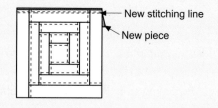
Pieced, Stuffed, and Appliquéd

Have you ever looked at a block design that appeared to be simple until you were already committed to doing it? That's just what happened during the construction of "What 'Marbelous' Tulips" (page 34). The problem was that the intersection of the appliquéd stem and the base of the tulip was bulky. In addition, only the main body of the tulip was to be stuffed with batting. After repeated unsuccessful attempts, the following solution was found.

1. Cut the background fabric to the desired size of the finished block, including seam allowances. Appliqué the stem to the background fabric.

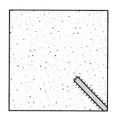

2. Piece the upper portion of the flower section. Press the ¼"-wide seam allowances under along the bottom edges of the flower.

3. Lay the pieced flower over the background fabric, aligning the stem with the base of the flower. Appliqué the 2 pressed edges to the background fabric.

4. Appliqué the leaves.

5. Stuff a small amount of batting under the flower.

6. Baste the 2 remaining open edges of the flower to the background fabric, within the ¼"-wide seam allowance. These basting stitches do not need to be removed later. Continue piecing your project.

Baste seam allowances closed after stuffing.

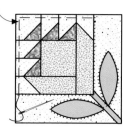

Pieced and Stuffed Tubes

Use this technique if you want to sew many pieces together, then turn them into a stuffed tube. See "Tubes" (page 37).

1. Cut each piece of fabric for the tube the same width.

2. Sew the pieces together end-to-end, using ¼"-wide seam allowances. Press the seams open to distribute the bulk. Carefully trim the seam allowances to ⅛".

3. Press under a ¼"-wide seam allowance on one long side of the pieced strip.

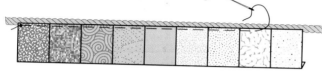

4. Baste the long, raw edge of the strip to a piece of cotton upholstery cording, wrong side of the fabric next to the cord. Cording can be purchased in a variety of widths and materials. Cotton cording grabs fabric better than nylon cording.

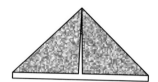

5. Roll the pieced strip around the cord, aligning the seam allowances of each piece.
6. Blindstitch the pressed edge along the full length of the tube.
7. Attach the tubes to your quilt with nylon filament. You can work from the back of the quilt so the stitches are not visible, or you can couch the tube from the front.

Reversed Fabric

As simple as it may sound, using the reverse side of your fabric can sometimes help you get the look or color you want. The reverse side of a fabric is often a lighter value of the color on the front. Sometimes it may be a shade darker, and sometimes the back of the fabric has almost no relationship to the front. The trick is to look at the wrong side and consider using it. Just think, you could double the number of your existing fabrics by using the reverse side! We used the reverse sides of fabrics in "Flip Side" (page 13) and "Stacked Cubes" (page 28) to achieve a three-dimensional look.

Sheer Overlay

A sheer fabric covers the fused center section of "Fusion" (page 31). Organza or any other sheer fabric can be used for this purpose. The sheer overlay diffuses the colors and softens the edges of the piecework underneath.

A sheer overlay can also be placed on sections of a quilt to simulate rays of light, or light and shadow. Since most sheer fabrics fray easily, they are virtually impossible to hand appliqué. Instead, baste the sheer fabric in place by hand, then machine appliqué the raw edge, using a zigzag stitch and invisible nylon thread.

Three-Dimensional Blossoms
Folded Buds

There are many ways to create three-dimensional flowers. The three-dimensional bud described here was developed for "Snapdragons" (page 21). The 100 buds in the vine border called for a quick assembly method. The use of a steam iron and a sewing machine makes these buds unique in shape and speedy in construction.

1. Cut a 1" x 1⅜" rectangle from each bud fabric. Press under ¼" on one long side as shown. Fold both top corners to the center and press.

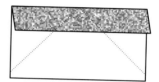

2. Fold this triangle in thirds and press again. Be sure to use steam when pressing the folds. This is the three-dimensional section of the bud.

3. Cut a strip of fabric for the bud bases. For the length, multiply 1¼" by the number of buds. (For example, 1¼" x 10 buds = 12½".) Pin the buds along this strip, right sides together, with a ⅝" space between each bud. Stitch ¼" from the raw edge of the strip.

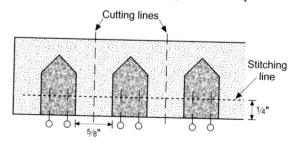

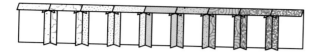

Flock of Geese Variation

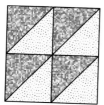
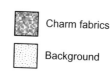

Charm fabrics

Background

Finished Block Size: 3"
See "Flocks of Geese": page 27
Templates: page 76

Cutting for One Block

From the charm fabrics, cut:
4 of Template D
From the background fabric, cut:
4 of Template D

Piecing Diagram

Make 4.

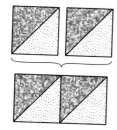

Make the appropriate number of blocks based on the number of fabrics in your master set. This pattern works well with master sets that are divisible by 4.

Charm Placement Options

Finishing Options

- "Flocks of Geese" features an unusual setting. It combines two additional blocks with the Flock of Geese variation to create a secondary pattern. For the half-square triangle blocks, use Template F.

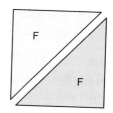

Half-Square Triangle Block

For quarter-square triangle blocks, use Templates E and F.

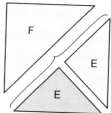

Quarter-Square Triangle Block

Make the appropriate number of alternate blocks for the number of Flock of Geese blocks you made from your master set. For example, to make the setting shown below, you need 25 Flock of Geese, 8 quarter-square, and 16 half-square triangle blocks.

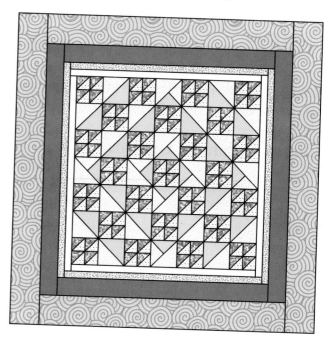

- Frame the quilt with multiple borders. Vary the texture and value of the fabrics to add interest.

Southpaw

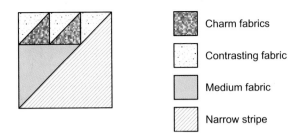

- Charm fabrics
- Contrasting fabric
- Medium fabric
- Narrow stripe

Finished Block Size: 4½"
See "Southpaw": page 33
Templates: page 76

Cutting for One Block

From the charm fabrics, cut:
　　2 of Template D
From the contrasting fabric, cut:
　　3 of Template D
From the medium fabric, cut:
　　1 of Template F
From the narrow stripe, cut:
　　1 of Template G

Piecing Diagram

Make 2.

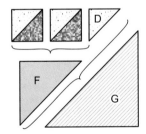

Make the appropriate number of blocks based on the number of fabrics in your master set. This pattern works well with master sets that are divisible by 2.

Charm Placement Options

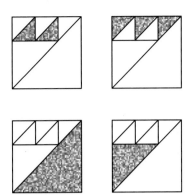

Finishing Options

- An on-point setting works well with this block.
- Use a striped fabric to create the illusion of depth. Careful placement of the templates on the fabric will enhance this effect.
- Try incorporating hand-dyed fabrics in your work. They add an interest other fabrics can't. Notice the effective use of gradated hand-dyed fabrics in "Southpaw." A series of lighter values was used in the small triangles. A series of medium values was used in the large triangles.
- The Southpaw block is actually one-quarter of a classic Rosebud block. Group 4 Southpaw blocks for a dynamic setting.

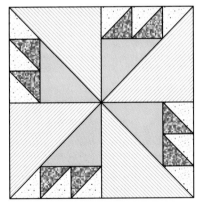

Rosebud

Peaks and Valleys

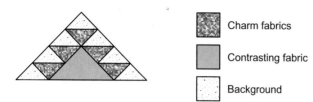

- Charm fabrics
- Contrasting fabric
- Background

Finished Block Size: 5"
See "Peaks and Valleys": page 30
Templates: pages 76–77

Cutting for One Block

From the charm fabrics, cut:
   5 of Template H
From the contrasting fabric, cut:
   1 of Template I
From the background fabric, cut:
   7 of Template H

Piecing Diagram

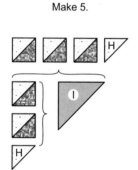

Make 5.

Make the appropriate number of blocks based on the number of fabrics in your master set. This pattern works well with master sets that are divisible by 5.

Charm Placement Options

Finishing Options

- Try using triangular blocks in more of your work. Set them with alternating plain triangles and piece them together to create rows.

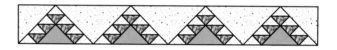

- The Peaks and Valleys block uses portions of the classic Delectable Mountains block and the Anvil block. When looking for designs to use in Ultimate Challenge quilts, examine blocks carefully to see if you can use just a portion.

Grandmother's Choice

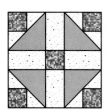

Charm fabrics

Medium or dark fabric

Background

Finished Block Size: 7½"
See "Grandmother's Choice": page 26
Templates: pages 76–77

Cutting for One Block

From the charm fabrics, cut:
    5 of Template J
From the medium or dark fabric, cut:
    4 of Template F
From the background fabric, cut:
    8 of Template D
    4 rectangles, each 2" x 3½"

Piecing Diagram

Make 4.

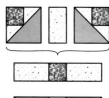

Make the appropriate number of blocks based on the number of fabrics in your master set. This pattern works well with master sets that are divisible by 5.

Charm Placement Options

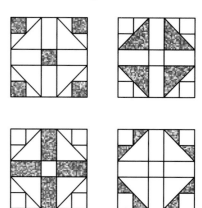

Finishing Options

- Use this block in a block-to-block straight set to create a secondary pattern and overlaying grid.
- Instead of using a single background fabric, use many fabrics of similar value (for example, all light). Select fabrics that have different visual textures when viewed from a distance. This adds subtle but distinctive dimension to your work.
- The following easy, small-scale quilting design can be adapted to any border length. Notice the difference between the two corners. The **S**-shaped curved unit can either *meet* (A) or *overlap* at the corner (B).

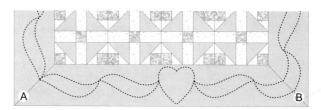

Milky Way Variation

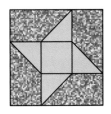

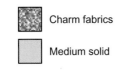
Charm fabrics

Medium solid

Finished Block Size: 3¾"
See "Milky Way": page 19
Templates: pages 76–77

Cutting for One Block

From the charm fabrics, cut:
    4 of Template K
From the medium solid, cut:
    4 of Template H
    1 square, 1¾" x 1¾"

Piecing Diagram

Make 4.

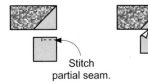

Stitch
partial seam.

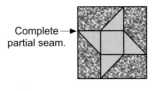
Complete
partial seam.

Make the appropriate number of blocks based on the number of fabrics in your master set. This pattern works well with master sets that are divisible by 4.

Charm Placement Options

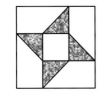

Finishing Options

- Referring to "Milky Way," notice the light-to-dark value change in the stars. This was accomplished with a set of eight gradated, hand-dyed fabrics. Check your local quilt shop and quilting-magazine advertisements for these wonderful fabrics.
- The diagram below shows a continuous line, machine-quilting design that repeats the star motif. Quilt the design on each border in 4 paths as shown.

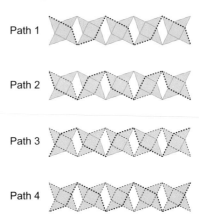
Path 1

Path 2

Path 3

Path 4

> **NOTE:**
> To create your own border design, select a motif or design element from the pieced section of your quilt top. Rotate and connect the element repeatedly to create a continuous linear design.

- Try floating the entire central design in an on-point set. Use one fabric for the side setting triangles, the corner triangles, and the first border, as in the night sky of "Milky Way."

Grandmother's Fan

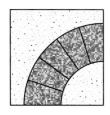

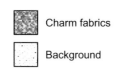
Finished Block Size: 6"
See "Fanatic": page 15
Templates: page 77

Cutting for One Block

From the charm fabrics, cut:
    5 of Template L
From the background fabric, cut:
    1 of Template M
    1 of Template N

Piecing Diagram

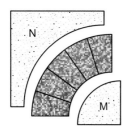

Make the appropriate number of blocks based on the number of fabrics in your master set. This pattern works well with master sets that are divisible by 5.

Charm Placement Options

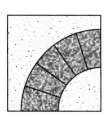

Pieces M and N are too large to be cut from most master sets, so this is the only practical placement option.

Finishing Options

- Consider using this unusual setting for 20 on-point blocks.

- Use strips of fabric that coordinate with your block fabrics to create a charming border. Combine these strips with shorter strips of dark background fabric. The length of each border can easily be adjusted to fit the center of the quilt. This border technique is both flexible and fun to do.

- Try some color clusters with this block. In "Fanatic," five charm fabrics were grouped by color for each fan. Base your selections primarily on color, but consider the value of each fabric as well.

Christmas Cactus Variation

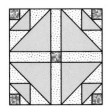

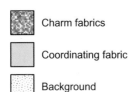

Charm fabrics

Coordinating fabric

Background

Finished Block Size: 13½"
See "Finally": page 44
Templates: pages 76–78

Cutting for One Block

From the charm fabrics, cut:
    5 of Template J
From the coordinating fabric, cut:
    4 of Template F
    4 of Template O
From the background fabric, cut:
    8 of Template D
    8 of Template F
    4 rectangles, each 2" x 6½"

Piecing Diagram

Make 4.

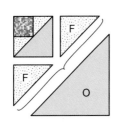

Make 4.

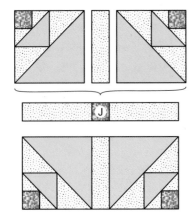

Make the appropriate number of blocks based on the number of fabrics in your master set. This pattern works well with master sets that are divisible by 5.

Charm Placement Options

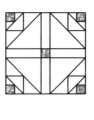

Finishing Options

- What makes "Finally" special is the large floral border. A single, wide border is particularly effective when the border print contains many of the colors found in the interior of the quilt.

- Floral clusters add charm to the alternate plain blocks of "Finally." To re-create this look, apply paper-backed fusible web to the wrong side of your large-scale floral fabric, and cut out single flowers or clusters of flowers. Arrange the flowers and greenery in different bouquets, and iron them in place. Machine appliqué the bouquets for stability, or leave the edges raw for a less defined look. Can you believe that all twelve floral clusters were cut from one border fabric? It's true. We wouldn't lie to fellow quilters.

- Create even greater variety in your blocks by using many fabrics. For example, cut Templates F and O for each quadrant from different fabrics. Coordinate your choices with the charm fabric in each quadrant.

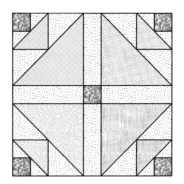

Snapdragons

Charm fabrics

Dark fabrics

Background

Finished Block Size: 4¾"
See "Snapdragons": page 21
Templates: pages 78–79

Cutting for One Block

From the charm fabrics, cut:
    4 of Template P
    4 of Template Q
From the dark fabric, cut:
    1 square, 1¾" x 1¾"
From the background fabric, cut:
    2 squares, each 1⅜" x 1⅜"
    2 rectangles, each 1⅜" x 2¼"
    2 rectangles, each 1⅜" x 3⅛"

Piecing Diagram

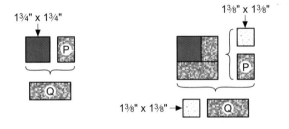

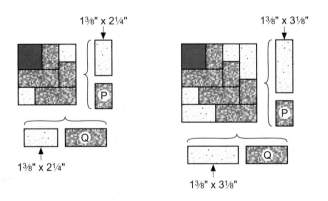

Make the appropriate number of blocks based on the number of fabrics in your master set. This pattern works well with master sets that are divisible by 4.

Charm Placement Options

Finishing Options

- "Snapdragons" is arranged in a complex on-point setting. Appliquéd bias strips and leaves create vines. A simplified setting with a similar look is shown below. It is composed of pieced blocks, plain blocks of the same size, and lattice strips. After piecing the center section, appliqué leaves and ⅜"-wide vines. Use the leaf template on page 79.

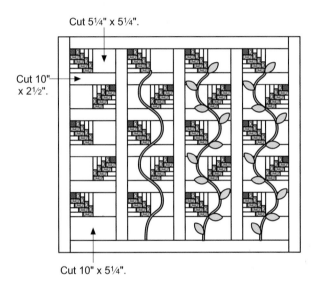

Cut 5¼" x 5¼".

Cut 10" x 2½".

Cut 10" x 5¼".

- Quilt a double-crosshatch pattern in the background to give the appearance of a trellis.

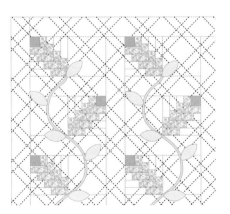

- Intricate appliqué borders like the three-dimensional buds and vines on "Snapdragons" can be a real challenge. Although time-consuming, borders of this type can enhance virtually any quilt top.

What "Marbelous" Tulips

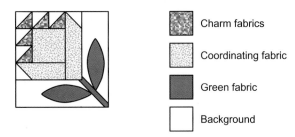

Charm fabrics

Coordinating fabric

Green fabric

Background

Finished Block Size: 7"
See "What 'Marbelous' Tulips": page 34
Templates: pages 76 and 78

Cutting for One Block

From the charm fabrics, cut:
    5 of Template H
From the coordinating fabric, cut:
    1 of Template R
    1 of Template U
    1 square, 3" x 3"
From the green fabric, cut:
    1 of Template S
    2 of Template T
From the background fabric, cut:
    7 of Template H
    1 square, 7½" x 7½"

Piecing Diagram

Make 5.

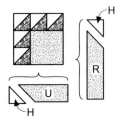

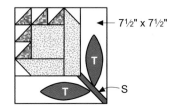

Make the appropriate number of blocks based on the number of fabrics in your master set. This pattern works well with master sets that are divisible by 5.

Refer to "Pieced, Stuffed, and Appliquéd" on page 56 to complete the block.

Charm Placement Options

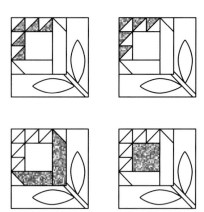

Finishing Options

- The following block-to-block straight set works well with 20 directional blocks. A directional block is one that has a definite top and bottom.

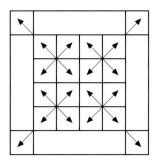

- Marbleized fabrics add wonderful texture. You can learn how to make your own marbleized fabrics from a book or by taking a class. If you don't like messy projects, look for marbleized fabrics at your local quilt shop.
- Try mimicking the pieced pattern with your quilting, as in the border of "What 'Marbelous' Tulips." If you set your blocks as shown, the quilting won't require fancy figuring and will fit the border perfectly.

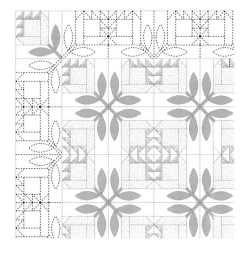

Chinese Fan

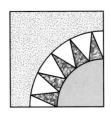

Charm fabrics

Coordinating fabric #1

Coordinating fabric #2

Background

Finished Block Size: 6"
See "Crown of Thorns": page 18
Templates: page 79

Cutting for One Block

From the charm fabrics, cut:
    5 of Template V
From coordinating fabric #1, cut:
    1 of Template Y
From coordinating fabric #2, cut:
    1 of Template Z
From the background fabric, cut:
    4 of Template X
    1 of Template W
    1 of Template W reversed

Piecing Diagram

Make 4.

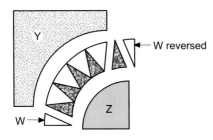

Make the appropriate number of blocks based on the number of fabrics in your master set. This pattern works well with master sets that are divisible by 5.

Charm Placement Options

Finishing Options

- Consider rotating blocks for a completely different look. This is another example of a directional block, like the one in "What 'Marbelous' Tulips " opposite. A block-to-block straight setting was used in both quilts. The difference between the two settings is the rotation of the center blocks. Look at both quilts and compare the results.

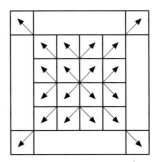

- Use many different coordinating fabrics when choosing "scraps." Truth be told, most of the scrap fabrics in "Crown of Thorns" were not random scraps at all, but deliberate choices. Choose fabrics that you really like—some of your favorites. You will like the end result, a scrappy look, if you dearly love the fabrics.

- Carry the pieced design through to the quilting design. Use pieced corner blocks in the border. Continue the pieced design with your needle by quilting it into the blank border, like this:

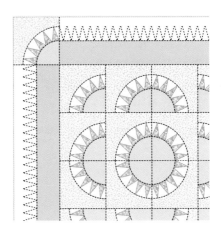

Other Ideas

If you have read through this book and like the idea, but aren't sure you want to accept the Ultimate Challenge, here are a few other possibilities.

- Use our quilts for inspiration. Look for a color combination that appeals to you, then select similar fabrics for your own quilt.

- Use a design or pattern we have tried, but modify it to make it uniquely yours.

- Collect charm squares for the fun of sorting them by color and keeping them in a pile. Who said you had to make a quilt from every piece of fabric you own? If this were true, we would be in big trouble.

- Challenge yourself to make a charm quilt using only fabrics that have objects, people, or animals on them. These prints, known as "conversation" prints, were popular in the late nineteenth and early twentieth centuries. It is amazing how many conversation prints are available today.

- Use many different background fabrics in one quilt to add variety and visual texture.

- Make only one quilt from your charm squares instead of a series of quilts. The quilt can include many of the Ultimate Challenge ideas without requiring such a large commitment.

- Make a charm quilt, but use only the charm squares you have already acquired. Although folklore says charm quilts should contain 999 different prints, we know otherwise. Only 323 five-inch squares, set 17 across by 19 down, make a quilt top that measures 76½" x 85½". That's the size of a twin blanket or a double-bed comforter.

- Try a new technique on your next project. Quiltmakers come up with new ways of doing things every day. Maybe the latest technique is one that suits you. When you have an idea in your head, figure out a way to get it onto fabric. If you read "Tips and Techniques" (pages 51–58), you'll see we tried almost anything to make our ideas a reality.

- Work in a series by creating two, three, or more quilts from the same set of fabrics. If you have a favorite quilt design, make it several times in different color combinations. It is amazing how different one quilt design can look with just a change of color.

- If the Ultimate Challenge is more than you want to take on, accept a different challenge. The next time your guild announces a new challenge or you see one in a quilt magazine, give it a try. Challenge quilts are usually small, and you need to make only one! The point is to push your quilting boundaries a little further with each quilt.

- Occasionally, fabric manufacturers challenge us to use some pretty wild fabrics. If the fabric in the latest challenge makes your eyes jump, use the rest of the rules, but change the fabrics. You won't be able to enter your quilt as part of the challenge, but you will still have fun making something new.

- Set up your own challenge. You can do this alone or with a group of friends. The fun is that you get to make up all the rules!

- Work on a miniature quilt. A small quilt can take just a few days instead of the months needed for a large piece. As we found out, "miniature" means different things to each quilter. Try working 50% smaller than you do now. If you usually make 12" blocks, try a few 6" blocks. After a few blocks, you might discover your perception of miniature has changed. Too small becomes just a little smaller than your last effort.

- Collaborate with a good friend on just one quilt. Plan to give your first joint effort to charity. This way, neither quilter feels a sense of possession, and ideas flow more freely. We made several charity quilts together before starting this project. Even if you just ask for a little input from one other person, you will have embarked on a new path. Sharing the quilting experience with a friend can be wonderful. Who knows, maybe your spouse, roommate, coworkers, or kids would like to toss in their two-cents worth.

- Think of a project you really want to do but have put off for whatever reason. Break it down into manageable pieces and set aside time to do the first piece. We have discovered you must make the time, not find the time. Schedule a meeting with yourself and don't let anyone or anything interfere. This is what we did in order to get this book written. Writing a book seemed like such a lofty goal, considering the commitments in our lives, but we just jumped in with both feet and kept running.

Block Ideas

The Ultimate Challenge will stretch your skills in many ways. Choosing the right block design becomes a challenge in and of itself. Detailed information about selecting block patterns is provided in "Accepting the Ultimate Challenge" on pages 49–51. When considering a block, look for the unit in the design where you can put the charm fabrics from your master set. The blocks you choose must incorporate the *exact* number of fabrics in your master set. Some blocks will work, some won't.

The blocks illustrated in this section are only a few of the possibilities. The highlighted units in each design indicate where the charm fabrics from your master set could be placed. You can put your fabrics in different units, depending on the effect you want.

There are literally thousands of block designs to explore with the Ultimate Challenge in mind. After accepting the Ultimate Challenge, you will never again look at a block in the same way.

Blocks for One Charm

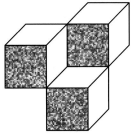

Box Quilt

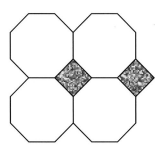

Octagon

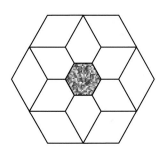

Hexagonal Star

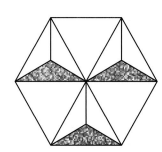

Wonder of Egypt

Blocks for Two Charms

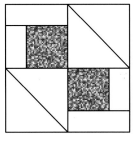

Picket Fence

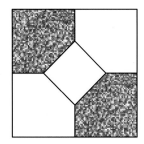

Bow Tie

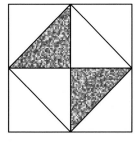

Broken Dishes

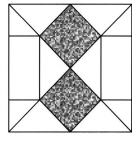

Boise, Idaho

Blocks for Three Charms

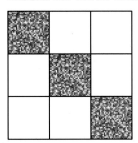

Nine Patch

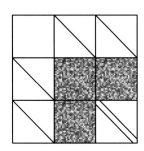

Maple Leaf

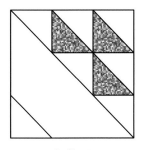

Sailboat

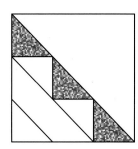

Golden Stairs

Blocks for Four Charms

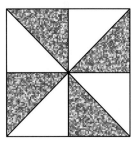

Crow's Foot

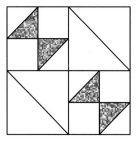

Crosses and Losses

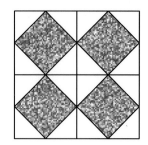

Broken Sash

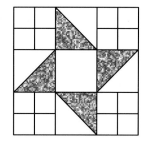

Water Wheel

Blocks for Five Charms

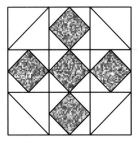

Sawtooth Patch

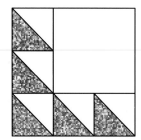

Birds in the Air

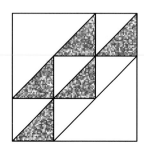

Northwind

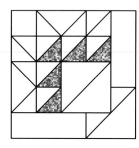

Grape Basket

Blocks for Six Charms

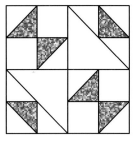

Old Maid's Ramble

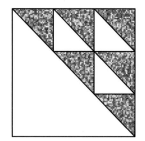

Flying Birds

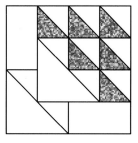

Basket

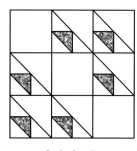

Cat's Cradle

Blocks for Eight Charms

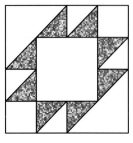

Anvil

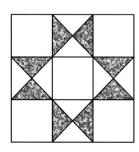

Ohio Star

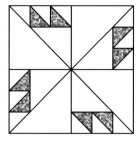

Rosebud

Spinning Stars

Blocks for Ten Charms

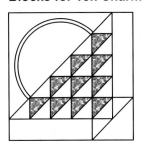

Cherry Basket

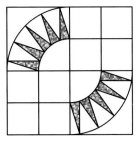

Dogwood Variation

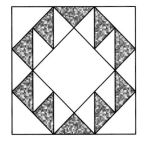

Jack's Delight

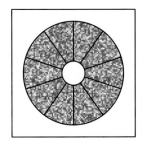

Baby Aster

Blocks for Twelve Charms

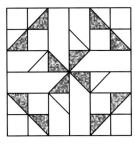

Contrary Wife

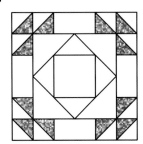

Double X

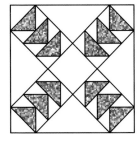

Wild Goose Chase

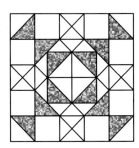

Hill and Crag

Blocks for Sixteen Charms

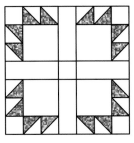

Bear's Paw

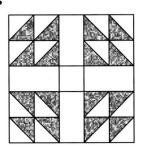

Handy Andy

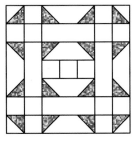

Greek Cross

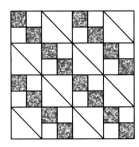

World's Fair

Appliqué Blocks

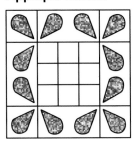

Honey Bee

Dresden Plate

The Posey Quilt

Wreath of Berries

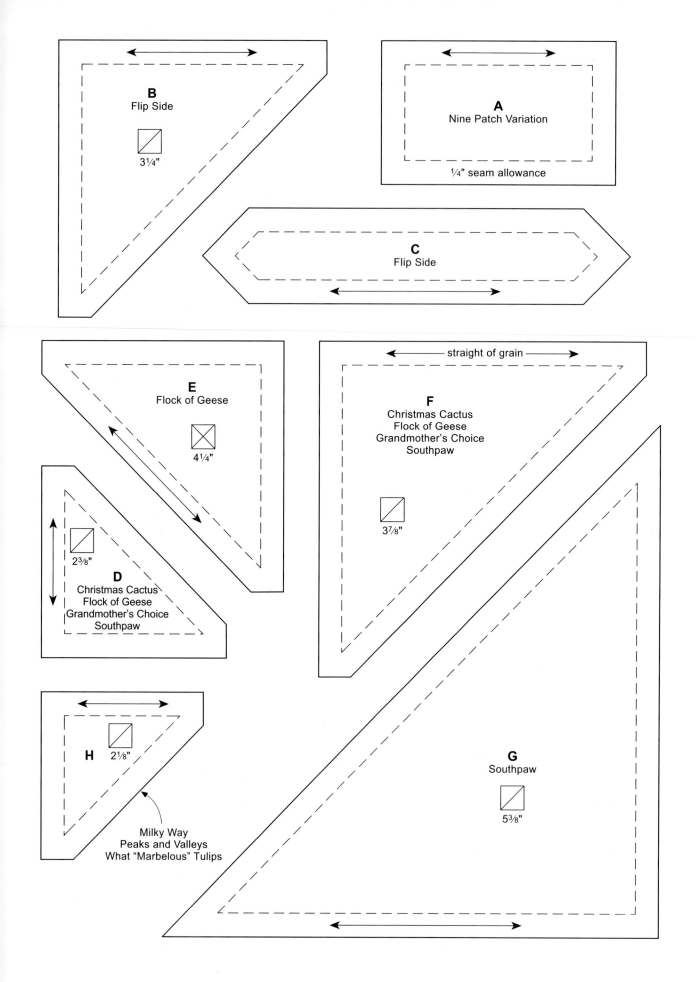

B
Flip Side

3¼"

A
Nine Patch Variation

¼" seam allowance

C
Flip Side

E
Flock of Geese

4¼"

straight of grain

F
Christmas Cactus
Flock of Geese
Grandmother's Choice
Southpaw

3⅞"

2⅜"

D
Christmas Cactus
Flock of Geese
Grandmother's Choice
Southpaw

H   2⅛"

Milky Way
Peaks and Valleys
What "Marbelous" Tulips

G
Southpaw

5⅜"

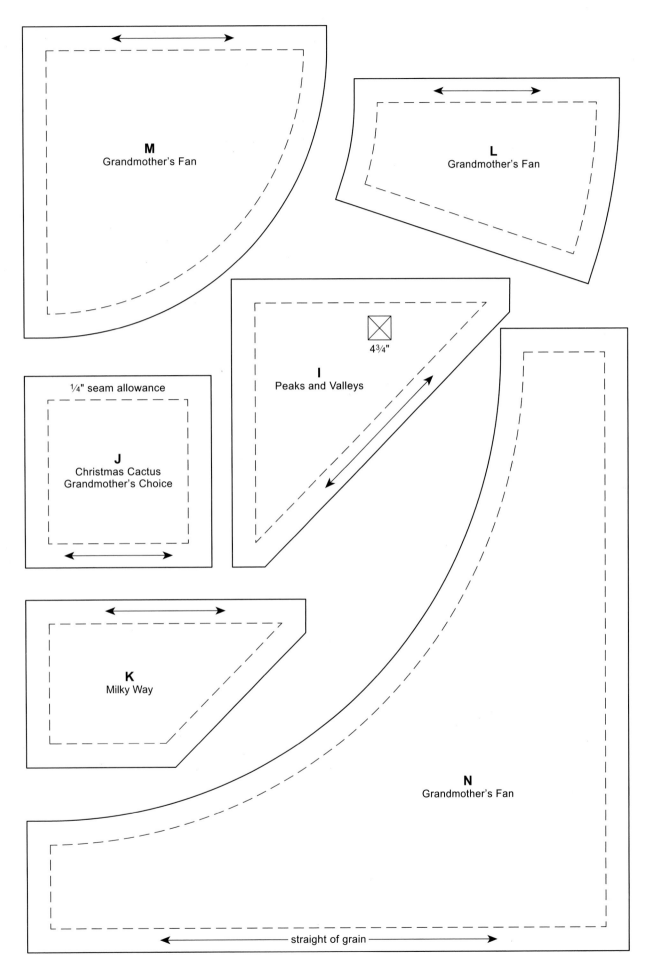

M
Grandmother's Fan

L
Grandmother's Fan

¼" seam allowance

J
Christmas Cactus
Grandmother's Choice

4¾"

I
Peaks and Valleys

K
Milky Way

N
Grandmother's Fan

straight of grain

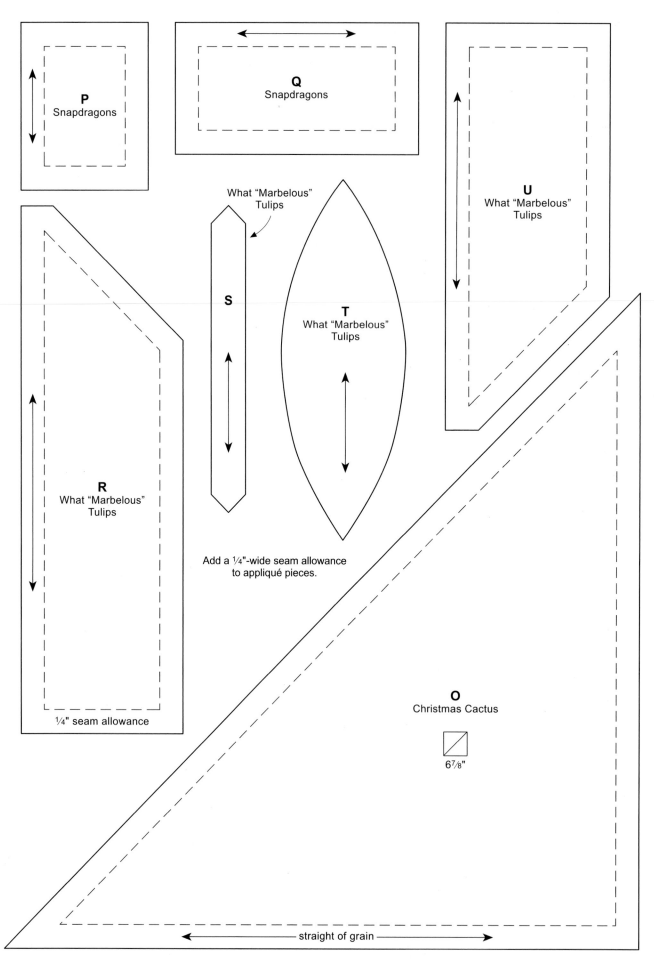

P
Snapdragons

Q
Snapdragons

U
What "Marbelous" Tulips

What "Marbelous" Tulips

S

T
What "Marbelous" Tulips

R
What "Marbelous" Tulips

Add a ¼"-wide seam allowance to appliqué pieces.

¼" seam allowance

O
Christmas Cactus

6⅞"

straight of grain

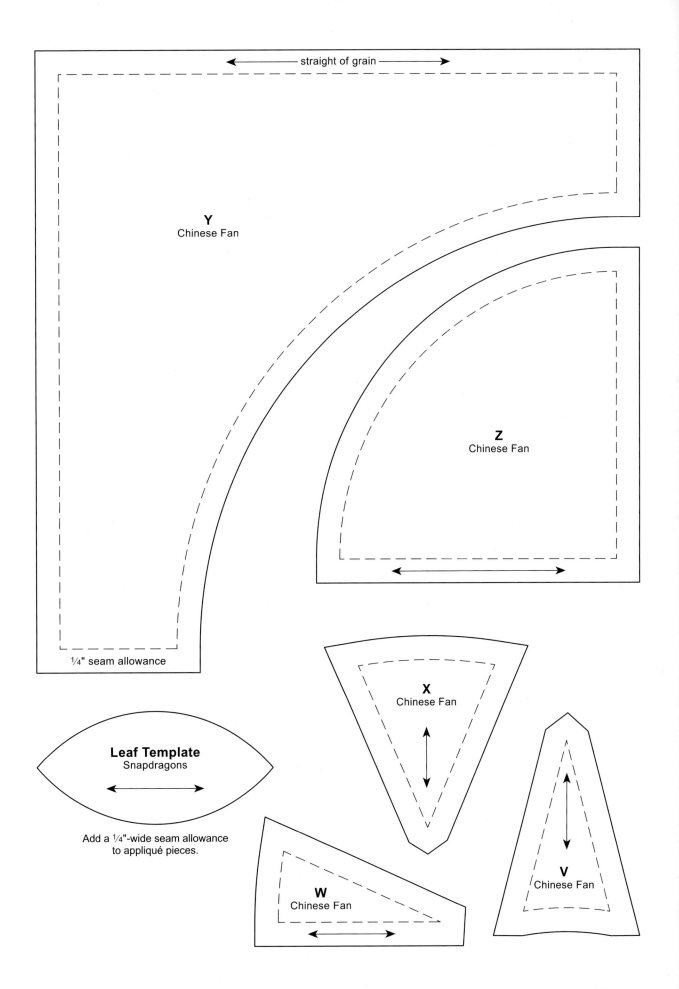

straight of grain

Y
Chinese Fan

¼" seam allowance

Z
Chinese Fan

Leaf Template
Snapdragons

Add a ¼"-wide seam allowance
to appliqué pieces.

X
Chinese Fan

V
Chinese Fan

W
Chinese Fan

About the Authors

While Cathy and Tammy both live in Troy, Michigan, and each has a husband and three children, they live very different lives. Cathy is a senior vice president of a large Midwestern bank, and Tammy works full time to raise her family. One thing they share is a passion for quilting. This all-consuming interest led them to collaborate on several other projects before they embarked on the Ultimate Challenge. They are living proof that no matter what your job or lifestyle, quilting goals can be accomplished if they are a priority.

Cathy and Tammy have been quilting for a combined total of thirty-five years. Their prize-winning quilts have been displayed both locally and nationally, and their work has been published in books and magazines. *Beyond Charm Quilts* is their first book.

Cathy and Tammy